TRUTH HAS A POWER
OF ITS OWN

TRUTH HAS A POWER OF ITS OWN

Conversations About
A People's History

HOWARD ZINN
WITH RAY SUAREZ

THE
NEW
PRESS

NEW YORK
LONDON

Requests for permission to reproduce selections from this book should be made
through our website: https://thenewpress.com/contact.

This book originated as an educational film project developed by The Independent
Production Fund and licensed for distribution to schools and libraries as a six-part
series under the title Howard Zinn: The People's Historian.

Published in the United States by The New Press, New York, 2019
Distributed by Two Rivers Distribution

ISBN 978-1-62097-517-6 (hc)
ISBN 978-1-62097-518-3 (ebook)
CIP data is available

The New Press publishes books that promote and enrich public discussion and
understanding of the issues vital to our democracy and to a more equitable world.
These books are made possible by the enthusiasm of our readers; the support of a
committed group of donors, large and small; the collaboration of our many partners
in the independent media and the not-for-profit sector; booksellers, who often hand-
sell New Press books; librarians; and above all by our authors.

www.thenewpress.com

Book design and composition by Bookbright Media
This book was set in Sabon and Univers

Printed in the United States of America

10 9 8 7 6 5 4 3 2 1

CONTENTS

When we organize with one another, when
we get involved, when we stand up and
speak out together, we can create a power no
government can suppress.

—Howard Zinn

This book is based on the transcripts of conversations between Howard Zinn and Ray Suarez that took place in 2007.

FOREWORD

In 2007, the phone on my desk at the *PBS NewsHour*, where I was a senior correspondent, rang as I was preparing for that night's broadcast. On the other end of the line was Al Perlmutter, documentary filmmaker, with an intriguing offer. He was contemplating a documentary on the life and work of Howard Zinn and needed someone to interview him. Was I interested?

How could I *not* be interested? In the endless tugs-of-war over what constitutes American history, the truth of what happened, and what we might conclude about this country's place in the world, Zinn had grabbed one end of the rope, and a lot of attention, for decades. His work was bracing, challenging, meant to force the reader into a new encounter with received ideas about the United States.

Now, near the end of his long career and, as it would turn out, of his long life, I would get a chance to pick the brain of my Brooklyn landsman. I asked Perlmutter about the time commitment. His plan was for us to talk for six hours over the course of two days. Six hours? For a daily deadline broadcaster, a ten-minute interview is long. For my books I might talk with a source for an hour, or if the conversation is crackling, energetic, unexpectedly fruit-ful . . . an hour and a half, tops. Could we sustain such long conversations without limping to the end like Depression-era marathon dancers trying to win a couple of bucks?

That was the last thing I needed to worry about.

Long, lean, crowned by a lion's mane of silver hair, Zinn bubbled over with ideas. In an austere old factory building in Queens, New York, we talked about the way Americans learn their history and why we learn what we do. We talked about the uses of history in creating a coherent narrative, and how people create meaning even around stories that are incomplete or untrue. My concerns about the project were laid to rest almost immediately, in the first minutes of conversation, after we began talking about one of the great exemplars of the historical flesh-and-blood figure encrusted over time with our need for heroes—Christopher Columbus.

I asked about the stories we've told each other over time about the Italian mariner–turned–Spanish colonial governor, and what the risks are in rewriting myths and reexamining heroes. Zinn's simple reply: "To break into this is to be a troublemaker."

Troublemaker is a role Zinn didn't shy away from. It is significant—and a sign of his own dogged, plainspoken approach—that in the years since the publication of *A People's History of the United States* in 1980, the text has moved from the fringes of the American conversation much closer to the center. Other "troublemakers" were of course also breaking into the American story . . . women, African Americans, Latinos and Latinas, sexual minorities, and so on. Time, arguments, and an increased willingness to debate, not only the plain facts of our national story but also what they mean, were moving the needle, leaving us, in Zinn's own words, ready "to rethink long-held ideas."

In the nearly forty years since the first edition of *A People's History* appeared, Zinn's critics have tried to sandbag him. Some complain that his iconoclasm, his tearing down of long-revered heroes, and his corrections to the record leave only a dreary slog through centuries of oppression, struggle, and suffering. Well, a historian's job is to find out what actually happened. The horrors are there all right, and Zinn is clear-eyed and persistent in forcing us to look at them.

Economic exploitation is never far from Zinn's mind as he recounts the history of the robber barons of the nineteenth century, the poor and working-class men of the South who took up arms for the Confederacy, the "girls" of the mill towns in Massachusetts who walked away from their machines to fight for better pay, the farmers driven to revolt by ruinous taxes on land. They all are characters in Zinn's American drama. Moving economics closer to the center of American history is more common today. In 1980, the lives and struggles of ordinary people had to muscle their way into the story to take up a place alongside generals on horseback, stirring words of historical documents, and Manifest Destiny.

However, in *A People's History* and later in *A Young*

People's History of the United States, as well as throughout the book you hold in your hands, right there along with the struggle and suffering is Zinn's idealism, embodied in a tableau vivant of new heroes along with the new perspectives. The historian wants to shatter your old notions about U.S. history. In the very same moment, he wants to remind you of the power of common people to challenge authority, improve their own circumstances, and change their country for the better.

The historian, the World War II veteran, the writer, the teacher is pulling on your sleeve again and again, saying, "Wait. There's more to this story. By filling out the picture, by shining a light on the dark corners, we're not tearing down your country. We're telling a more complicated story. We're telling, as a result, a more interesting story. In short, we're telling you the truth." In the interview you're about to read and throughout his published work, Zinn does not hesitate when it is required to tell a fuller truth about our country's supposed heroes.

Pick up a typical U.S. history textbook and you'll find celebrations of Theodore Roosevelt. Howard Zinn instead focuses on his bellicosity and racism. By contrast, during Martin Luther King Jr.'s public life and after his assassination, his detractors sought to use the civil rights leader's personal foibles to undermine his moral authority. Zinn takes a different approach. Discussing King's life, Zinn said, "What all people have in common is flaws and contradictions. What they don't have in common is that some people are not admirable in their relationship to society. Some people are acquirers of wealth and makers of war. And other people are people like King, who struggle for justice and speak out against war. It is those differences that are crucial in assessing human beings."

It is a time of striking division in the United States, not only over history, but also over what this country's role should be in the twenty-first century. Zinn is asking not only for a reckoning with the past, but for a reimagining of America's future as a nation among nations.

For Zinn, an honest look at who we were leads to an honest look at who we are. My career as a reporter took me to every corner of this country and to much of the world, and by vocation and inclination I've always believed that the complete picture is required. At the same time, I was a child of the Cold War, taught an idealized version of our history. Coming to *A People's History* as an adult, it was still a challenge to leave behind my belief in American exceptionalism. As Zinn said, "We have to start thinking of America as one among many, as a nation of people equal to other peoples but not superior to them. What that would do, aside from being an enormous psychological change for Americans, would be to bring about an honest recognition of who we are and what our limitations are, without denigrating ourselves."

I did not get the sense during our hours of conversation, and have not in all the years since, of anything Pollyanna-ish about this assessment. I concluded that Zinn's vision, toward the end of a life that stretched from the Roaring Twenties to the Age of the Internet, was more prescriptive than predictive. Political scientists, historians, and economists have spent the first decades of this still-young century trying to wrestle with the historical residue of an unrivaled American power that was the accidental result of the carnage and destruction of World War II. If you were born an American any time after 1945, you might have grown up with deeply ingrained assumptions about this country's place in the world that have proven pretty impervious to the "rise of the rest," as places like China, India, Brazil, Mexico, and Indonesia have become home to the world's largest economies.

It is hard to know how many of his fellow citizens would look favorably upon Zinn's prescription of a more humble and collaborative United States in the twenty-first century. Home to an increasingly diverse polyglot population of some 330 million, the nation is becoming a harder place to generalize about. Think of it: How would you complete the following sentences? Americans are ____. Americans want ____. Americans think ____. In the age of President Trump, we are having uncomfortable, even shocking conversations about how to fill in those blanks. In 1587, the birth of Virginia Dare represented a beginning of the European population of North America. The U.S. Census Bureau now forecasts the mid-2040s as the time when the birth of a darker-skinned child will swing the pendulum the other direction. In the lifetimes of many of you preparing to read this work, Americans whose ancestors come from Asia, Africa, and Latin America will outnumber those whose forebears came from Europe.

Howard Zinn was ready for that next America, and that next world.

Are you?

—*Ray Suarez*

TRUTH HAS A POWER
OF ITS OWN

PART I

"Change the Story": American Beginnings

What does it tell you that the received story of Colum-
bus, the conventional story of Columbus, the one that
we teach elementary school kids and high school kids,
doesn't include the genocide of the indigenous Caribbean
people?

Well, the absence of the real story of Columbus is due to a number of things. Probably the main reason for the distortion of the Columbus story is the desire for safety, the desire not to say anything that will be troublesome. After all, his statues appear in cities all over the country; cities are named after him, my university, Columbia University, and so on. I mean, he's a great American hero. To break into this is to be a troublemaker.

The first chapter of *A People's History of the United States* was on Columbus. When it was published, I soon began getting letters about the book from readers all over the country. And I noticed that most of the letters were about the very first chapter, about Columbus. First I thought, *Oh, they've only read the first chapter.* But then I thought, *No, this is the most shocking thing to them*— because it breaks into the American myth about Columbus. It has something to do with feeling that Columbus represents America, patriotism, Western civilization.

It's untouchable—you mustn't touch the myth about the glories of Western civilization, about the wonderful things that Europeans brought to other parts of the world. You mustn't touch the traditional heroes and make things more complicated than they are.

Four hundred years after Columbus, 1892, there was the quadricentennial celebration. An industrialist named Chauncey Depew gave a talk at Carnegie Hall to celebrate it. He said that to celebrate Columbus was to celebrate civilization as opposed to barbarism, and how it was wound up with patriotism. He himself was a great, great supporter of Theodore Roosevelt.

And Theodore Roosevelt, you might say, was the Columbus of his time. I don't know if anybody else has made that comparison, but I will anyway at this moment.

Roosevelt was an expansionist who believed in spreading the glories of Western civilization, first to the people of Cuba and then to the people of the Philippines.

So when you break into that story you are touching on things very sacred to the mythology and very sacred to people in power. People who are in charge of government have generally been people who, like Theodore Roosevelt, have favored the idea of Western expansion into what they consider uncivilized territory. So you might say it's kind of daring for teachers to change the story.

But does this have to be a binary function, so that if you revisit a hero or, as you put it, break into that story, does it have to be that you take a hero and turn him into a villain, or is there a way to fill in that story that tells you about Columbus for who he really was, puts him in his times, and makes us understand also a very human beginning to this encounter between Europe and the New World.

I agree that it is important to present it as a complicated picture—but not too complicated. We wouldn't tell a complicated story about Adolf Hitler. I'm saying there are people who played a certain role in the world that, when you examine it closely, is not a very humane role.

So Columbus is therefore a villain—or is there a way of telling history that just fills in those missing parts of the portrait and puts someone in their times?

Well, when I talk about Columbus, I don't ignore the fact that he was a brave man, that he was a great navigator, that he did something remarkable in crossing the ocean. That's one side.

But then there is the other side of him, the man who came here not to spread Christianity or care for people who were here, but to use them—use them in his search for gold, to bring profits to people back in Europe. A man who in that pursuit kidnapped Indians, mutilated them, killed them—enslaved them. Yes, you can humanize him. You can tell as much as you can about what he did that was positive or what his good personal qualities were, but in the end, if a person has committed atrocities, you make a judgment about that. The result is not simply "on the one hand, but on the other hand." It's not an equalization of the moral judgment—that is, if you have a moral approach to history.

If you don't believe in simply laying out history like a telephone book, if you believe that moral judgments should determine your approach to history, then I think you have to make decisions. You can tell the story of Theodore Roosevelt as a complicated story. You acknowledge there are remarkable things about him, and you can say, yes, he was a great lover of nature. He overcame enormous physical handicaps, and in fact, as president, he put in certain reforms.

But on the other hand, there is Roosevelt the lover of war. There is Roosevelt the imperialist. There is Theodore Roosevelt the racist. There is the Roosevelt who commends a general for committing a massacre in the Philippines.

You could say the good things about Theodore Roosevelt, but in the end, if your concerns are human concerns, then you have to make a decision about what else you tell. In a certain sense, you are filling in the picture. You are more truthful. You're not leaving things out, but you're putting things in that have been left out—things that are very, very important.

So if you took your view as laid out in A People's History *and revisited many of these personalities—Columbus, the Roosevelts—would we be changing the name of Columbus, Ohio? Would we be taking down the statues in Columbus Circle? Would we be delisting Columbus Day as an national holiday?*

Well, as a matter of fact, there have been campaigns in a number of states to do away with Columbus Day. The Dakotas renamed Columbus Day to Native American Day, and I remember there being parades in Colorado calling for Columbus Day to have its name changed. It is very hard to take down the statues of Columbus, wherever they are. The important thing is not so much these artifacts. *The important thing is to tell the truth.* I would take young people to the statue of Columbus not in order to tear it down but to say, "Here, now I'm going to tell you the truth about Columbus."

Should we be de-emphasizing that kind of narrative that's built around heroes in age to age to age?

I think we should be de-emphasizing the attention paid in traditional history to great military heroes, to presidents, to Supreme Court justices, to members of Congress, because our history generally has been history pulled from the top down. It has been the history of what the people on top do. In fact you can see that reflected in journalism today, where the people who fill the television screens are the president and the secretary of defense, and the press conferences of the people in government and the congressmen and so on.

I wanted to tell the story of other people, of people who perhaps were victimized by the presidents and the military heroes, here and abroad. I wanted to bring these ordinary people into the picture and maybe to create new heroes, or at least to talk about heroism in a different way. Heroism becomes a matter of who did the right thing. Then Rosa Parks becomes a hero. Then Bob Moses, a young fellow who goes into Mississippi in the 1960s to organize black people—then he becomes a hero. Fannie Lou Hamer, who is not too well known to most Americans, a Mississippi woman, a sharecropper who became a leader in the struggle for equal rights—she becomes a hero.

Helen Keller is already a hero, but in a way that eliminates what I think she should be admired for. Now, Helen Keller is a hero in our schoolbooks because she was a kid suffering under these great disabilities who became a famous person, a writer, even a speaker, even though she couldn't speak at first. But what is omitted from the story is that Helen Keller was a moral crusader against the war. She spoke out against World War I, spoke out for the rights of labor. She became a Socialist. She even joined the picket line on a theater that was showing a play about her. It is troublesome to me that there are people who are heroes but who are made heroes for the wrong reasons or for inadequate reasons. Mark Twain is a heroic figure in literature, and everybody who studies American literature or American history knows about Mark Twain as a great novelist. But how many people are taught in our schools or in our books that Mark Twain was a leader of the Anti-Imperialist League at the turn of the century? That he spoke out against the invasion of the Philippines?

So, yes, let's have heroes, and heroines, but let's look for them in different places than on high in the seats of power where the heroism very often consists of exploiting other people or invading other people or taking advantage of other people. Let's look for heroism among people who struggle at great odds against authority, very often against government, for justice and equality.

If we are to paint this more nuanced picture of American history and add Dorothy Day, maybe put her por-

trait up right next to Henry Ford's, do we end up with
a usable history?—what theorists have sometimes called
a usable history, wherein one of the ways French people
know they're French is the Frenchness that they get from
what they're taught in their history books, just as Ameri-
cans know they're American by what they believe about
American history.

They still get American history in the history I'm talking about, but it's a different kind of history with a different approach. It says something very important to the
person studying it. It says these are the models of what
a good human being should be doing. This person is the
kind of person you should want to emulate—this person
who struggled against racial inequality, fought against
war, or struggled for women's rights. Or this person like
Dorothy Day, who lived a very simple life and believed in
nonviolence. It's still history. It's just a different kind of
history.

It's a history, I think, that makes the listener, the reader,
the imbiber of history, more of a human being and also
more of an active person. If the heroes are the important
decision makers, all you have to do as a citizen is to go
to the polls every two or four years, pull down the levers,

and elect another savior. But now if you take this other set of heroes, your role as a citizen is not simply to vote but to become an active person in a movement for social justice. It's not just voting once every few years. It means every day becoming part of some social movement that wants to make the country and the world better.

*   *   *

One of the names that rises up from this different way of teaching is Olaudah Equiano, a name that a lot of Americans haven't heard. Why should we learn about Equiano today in twenty-first-century America?

Well, Olaudah Equiano suggests there must be a lot of people out there, and maybe important people, who have been kept from us.

Equiano was there, in the slave ships. We have very, very few firsthand reports of what happened in those slave ships that first brought slaves to Latin America in the sixteenth and seventeenth centuries, and then to North America. He describes the slave ships in a way that makes us understand the history of black people coming to this continent, makes us understand it in the most penetrating and disturbing way. After all, white people *should* be disturbed by that history, because if we're not disturbed by it, we'll be complacent. We'll say, "Oh well, you know black people have made a lot of progress, and there's no need to do anything special on the race question, because everything's okay now." But if we knew that history, we would know there's a very deep and long history of cruelty in this country. That history is something that still lives with black people and still affects their lives.

Equiano writes one of the earliest memoirs of transportation from Africa—in chains, his life as property. It's a sensation among that fraction of the public that is the reading public of the eighteenth century, but it doesn't lead to a clamor to end the transatlantic slave trade. Is there a lesson in the fact that it doesn't prick the conscience of the average American, just that of an elite slice of America?

That is true, and this is very often the lack of progress or slowness of progress in social reform. The movement to abolish slavery takes a very long time. It's a slow awakening. You're right—most people were deaf to all of this. First, a small number of people become abolitionists. After all, there is slavery not just in the South, but also in the North, right up through the American Revolution. There is slavery throughout the country. And the number of abolitionists is very small.

In the 1820s and 1830s, the number grows. Between 1830 and 1860 the number grows astronomically. That is a period when ex-slaves like Frederick Douglass and Harriet Tubman become leaders of the abolitionist movement, along with white abolitionists like Wendell Phillips and William Lloyd Garrison. A relatively small number of people in the 1830s call slavery to the attention of the entire country. And they do it very often by acts of civil disobedience, acts like those in the Southern movement that Martin Luther King and the Student Nonviolent Coordinating Committee committed in the 1960s. That is, they marched and they paraded, they broke into places, they violated the law. These abolitionists would barge into courthouses, into jailhouses, to rescue slaves who had run away from slavery, who are now in the North but are going to be sent back to slavery by the federal government, following the passage of the Fugitive Slave Act of 1850.

So in the early 1850s you find abolitionists in various parts of the country doing these very daring things, rescuing slaves in Boston and Pennsylvania, and in Antioch, Ohio, and in upstate New York. Sometimes they fail, and the slaves are brought back by armed force. But this brings the issue to the attention of the country. There is nothing that arouses attention so much as people who break a law.

That is why civil disobedience is such a powerful weapon in the hands of social reformers. And it's interesting that very often these people who rescued the slaves were apprehended and put on trial, and then juries, white jurists, would find them not guilty. Which meant that by this time antislavery feeling had reached into the general population. So it is a long process, from Equiano to the abolitionists of the mid-nineteenth century to, finally, the Thirteenth Amendment.

Does it change how we look at Equiano, how we understand him—to know that with some of the wealth that he enjoyed from writing an international bestseller, he invested in farms in the Caribbean that sought to use slave labor?

Well, it would change our personal estimate of Equiano, but it wouldn't change the importance of what he had to say. People are complicated. And there's nothing wrong with showing those complications but at the same time understanding that his narrative of his experience is an enormously important contribution to our understanding of the slave trade.

So it's like Bartolomé de las Casas, for instance, who blew the whistle on Columbus, who exposed what Columbus and the Spaniards did to the Tainos, told about their cruelties. And las Casas himself was no saint. At one time he held slaves and land. But I think, while accepting that about him, the important thing is to recognize his contribution. And in a more simple sense, almost everybody who makes some important contribution to the advance of human rights has something wrong with them.

* * *

There was slavery on every inhabited continent of the world at one time or another. There were thousands of years of history of slavery leading up to the seventeenth, eighteenth, and nineteenth centuries in the United States. However, you suggest in your book that American chattel slavery was something very different and worse than slavery anywhere else. Why?

Well, there was slavery in Africa, and the conditions were different, the restrictions were different. It seems strange to say that the slaves were treated more like human beings, because you think in slavery you simply aren't a human being, but there are degrees of cruelty in the treatment of slaves.

A million slaves had been brought to Latin America and the West Indies during the hundred years before slavery even began in North America. And in these places, very often, the slaves' families were recognized as families— they weren't broken up. They were given more rights as human beings. A number of people have compared slavery in these various places. American slavery was especially harsh and cruel in its dehumanization of the black person in this country.

Throughout the Western Hemisphere, but especially in North America, was it necessary to create a rationale for slavery that made its continuation possible? Did you have to sort of create a cultural argument for the black person as a slave in order to keep the whole thing going?

Racism is the creation of a certain attitude toward people to show that they are not as deserving of freedom as other people—that there is something different about them. What is different is not just the color of their skin or the shape of their features; what is different about them is that they are inferior human beings. Sometimes the inferiority is put in religious terms: "They're not Christians. They're heathens." And sometimes the differences are cast as a matter of intelligence, that the black person is not as intelligent as the white person, or that the black person is more savage and more cruel than the white person, or that black people are cannibals. All sorts of rationales are given for making the slave deserving of slavery—because they're not simply human beings like the rest of us.

This starts early. It starts with Columbus and the enslavement of Indians, in fact with the people who defended the enslavement of Indians at the time of Columbus—Juan Ginés de Sepúlveda, for instance, a Spanish priest who defended the cruel treatment of Indians. He did it by saying, well, they're simply a different species than we are; they're not really human beings. But las Casas lived among them and knew them and could talk about them. He said, no, they are human beings just like us. In fact, in some ways they're superior human beings in the way they behave toward one another, their attitude toward acquisition of property, and their belief in sharing things.

But it was necessary to create a myth about the inferiority of black people in order to justify enslaving them. And that myth, of course, has persisted for a long time.

*   *   *

As the Spanish empire encounters the native peoples of South America and the Caribbean, other parts of Europe encounter the indigenous nations of North America. Up in New England, for example, how does the Pequot Massacre fit into the narrative of the northern European foothold on our continent?

The Pequot Massacre takes place in 1637 in New England, on Block Island. It's one of the first elements in a very long history that is fundamentally about the white settler wanting more land. Wanting the materials of the land. Wanting gold in Georgia, wanting oil in Oklahoma (though that's later on). At first just wanting the land—the land that the Indians live on. So the massacres start early.

When the Indians retaliate to the massacres, it's considered terrorism.

It was massacre after massacre in New England, and

all justified: justified by the Church, by Cotton Mather, a leading theologian of New England, who is happy that six hundred Pequots were, as he puts it, "sent down to hell in that incident."

And the massacres continue. The massacres continued in New Amsterdam—New York State when the Dutch were in control, before the English came in. The wars against the Indians continue all through the eighteenth and nineteenth centuries. It's a very long history. It's history that's largely untold. That is, if you look at the treatment of our relations with Indians in the American history textbooks, it is a very flimsy treatment.

Did their status as religious and political refugees make the first Europeans in New England sympathetic to the people that they found already living there when they arrived?

Well, unfortunately not. Because the people who were already living here were standing in the way of what the newcomers wanted. They wanted to settle on land already lived on by Indians. So there was an inevitable clash between people who had come here wanting land—*needing* land, really, looking at it sympathetically from the point of view of the people coming—and the Indians already here. This clash continued all through American history.

The American Revolution was an important turning point, because the Indians had been given a certain amount of security when the British were in charge of the colonies. The British had set a line and the settlers could not move westward beyond that line into Indian territory. But when the British were driven out by the American Revolution and the colonists won their independence, that barrier—established by the Proclamation of 1763—was done away with.

The rest of the eighteenth and nineteenth centuries is a history of white Americans moving into Indian territory with enormous amounts of violence, massacre after massacre. The Indians were looked upon in the same way that the black slaves were looked upon, as inferior human beings. Uncivilized. They didn't understand what civilization was, and so they had to give way to the white person.

A lot of the early history of the European incursion, that westward move, is a story of negotiation, settlement, purchase, but then it gives way at various points of tension to massacre. How do you go from talking to somebody about how we're both going to live on this land to then just killing?

Well, what happens is, treaties are signed, and then treaties are broken. The colonists signed treaties with just a few Indians who were leaders and agreed to the terms, but then the rank and file of the Indians wouldn't go along with it. And very often the white Americans found that the treaty confined them too much, that they wanted this land that they had agreed to give to the Indians. You see this again and again.

In the 1830s, under Andrew Jackson and then his successor Martin Van Buren, the military moved against the Indians in the southeastern United States in what was officially called, in the title of the law authorizing it, Indian Removal. Today we'd call it ethnic cleansing. It was a process of the army moving down into Georgia and herding the Indians together—the Cherokees of Georgia, and then the Creeks, and the Choctaws, and the Chickasaws, and the Seminoles—and driving them westward through Georgia, through Alabama, through Mississippi, across the Mississippi River. The Trail of Tears took place at that time, in which sixteen thousand Indians were driven westward, with the army surrounding them and at their backs. In the course of this trek westward, four thousand of the sixteen thousand died.

This is a part of Indian history that I did not learn in school. I learned about Custer's Last Stand. I learned about Buffalo Bill. But I did not learn about Indian Removal. I learned that Andrew Jackson was a hero, a Democrat. I didn't learn that he was a killer of Indians, that he broke his promises to the Indians and that their fate was to be driven out of their land.

This quest for more and more land continues throughout the nineteenth century. The untold story of the Civil War is that part of the Union Army, instead of fighting the Confederacy, was sent out west to take Indian land. More Indian land was taken from them in the years of the Civil War than in any comparable period in American history. In 1864 in Colorado, the Sand Creek Massacre took place, where hundreds of Indian villages were simply attacked by the American army and annihilated.

This is the part of American history that Indians know today, and they become embittered when they find that most other Americans do not know this history, do not understand what happened to them. But it is part of modern history, of the history of Western nations expanding into other people's lands and committing great acts of violence in order to secure this land.

There is an interesting comment made in 1885 by Henry Dawes, the senator who was the author of the Dawes Act. Under the Dawes Act, the government forcibly surveyed tribal lands, took away the communal property from Indians, and broke the lands up into smaller holdings for private ownership.

Dawes visited Indian territory and was shocked by what he saw. He said these Indians don't know what civilization is. They don't hold on to private property—they *share* things. They don't understand—and this is the word he used—*selfishness*. He complained that among them, "There is no selfishness, which is at the bottom of civilization."

Well, this was the attitude toward the Indians. They did not understand about private property. They thought property should be communal. Therefore they did not fit into the civilization that was represented by the white person coming into this land.

* * *

Do we have to be careful not to make the mistake of turning the indigenous residents of North America into plaster saints, noble savages, people who never had an untoward thought or an unkind feeling? Didn't they also, as Europeans did, as Asians did, fight centuries of wars to settle territory, to expand political and economic control over swaths of what became the United States?

Well, there *were* Indian tribes that fought one another, and there were Indian tribes that committed massacres against white settlers who came into their territory. So to glamorize the Indians or to make them perfect would be a terrible mistake. But at the same time, it is very important to recognize what almost every close observer of Indian life saw and what they wrote about again and again. This starts with the Jesuit priests of the sixteenth century who came into the Western Hemisphere and observed how Indians live.

It starts with las Casas, who observes the Indians of the Caribbean. And then it continues with people who observe how the Iroquois were living in the northeastern territories. And what all of them report is that the Indians have a different way of life than the white man.

And yes they will go to war and they will commit

massacres, but their way of life—their normal way of life is a way of sharing, one in which women are treated much better in Indian society than women are treated in white Western society.

And all these observers talk about people being gentle. It starts with the Indians that Columbus encountered and he records this in his diary. He says they are the most gentle people in the world. They don't know about arms. They don't know what swords are. And they share things, they give things. It *is* a complicated picture, but I think what to look for when you're telling history is whatever part of this complicated picture is most ignored.

I think what is most ignored is the fact that the kind of life that the Indians lived actually had so many of the qualities that many people today in modern times long for—that is, a life without ferocious competition. So it's important to learn about that. It's important to learn about how the drive for material goods, for gold, for oil, for land, sends nations in modern times into very bloody wars of conquest.

* * *

Let's go back to the seventeenth century and Virginia Colony and another less-told story of history, Bacon's Rebellion. It's useful to shine a light on it as you do, in A People's History, *but one thing that jumped out at me was how, in this pungent stew of European gentry, European working class and peasantry, Indians, and newly arrived black people, there was so little fellow feeling among the have-nots. While they all shared a view of the haves as a common enemy, they never saw a common cause as a way to fight it.*

Well, you know, it's a very common thing in history that people who are victims will turn upon one another. Very often it's because the other that they turn upon is close at hand and because they can't reach the powerful. They can't reach the people who are really responsible for their plight, so they turn on those who are closest to them. We've seen this in the American South, the poor whites who have nothing turning against black people. The real source of their trouble is unreachable, and so this happens. It happens with whites against black people. It happens with whites against Indians.

But it's also interesting that there *are* certain times when their humanity comes through, that is, a fundamental recognition that other people are like them when they find common cause. This is not an easy thing to attain, because all of the power in the established authority works to keep people apart and set them against one another.

Bacon's Rebellion, in 1676, exactly one hundred years before the Declaration of Independence, is an interesting example in which, momentarily, white servants and black slaves came together against the government of Virginia. Of course, part of their coming together was against Indians. One of their grievances was that they had not been protected enough against the Indians by the government of Virginia. So it was a very complicated and odd situation, but it is one where black people and white people got together in a common struggle against authority.

In the context, though, of what you call a chain of oppression.

That's right. Here are white colonists oppressed by England, and here are the black people oppressed by the whites. This is how oppression works, in a kind of chain of people who oppress one another, making it difficult to break that chain and disturb the situation. But every once in a while that disturbance does take place. Bacon's Rebellion was one of those.

One of the important things about Bacon's Rebellion is that it showed something about the class struggle that has always existed in this country, the struggle between the rich and the poor. Because what we are told in our history, very often, is that we are all united against some common enemy. All whites are united against Indians in the Indian wars. All colonists in the American Revolution are united against England.

But that is a falsification of a much more complex story in which, for instance, in the Revolutionary War, the white people of the colonies are not united against England. They are divided. There are people who are eager to declare independence from England, and there are other people who are not enthusiastic about it at all. Washington has a very hard time putting together an army. He finds that people down South have no particular interest in this revolution. He sends Nathanael Greene, one of his generals, down South to round up people and get them into the army, and he had to punish people who would not enlist.

Before the Revolution there is continual class conflict

in the colonies between poor whites and rich whites. Between tenants and landlords. Between people who have nothing, who are continually struggling to make a living, and the rich. There is a concentration of wealth in the colonies before the Revolution.

It's important to know that before the Revolutionary War there is such a long history of class conflict among the colonists. You have a bread riot in Boston, where people who are hungry break into warehouses for bread. You have poor farmers in North Carolina just before the Revolution rebelling against the government. You have tenants being put in jail for nonpayment of rent and then mobs surrounding the jail and releasing the tenants.

So in Bacon's Rebellion you have this uprising of the have-nots, and once faced with this situation the Virginia governor, the Virginia legislature—they do what? Well, one thing they do is, they recognize that Bacon's Rebellion is a popular rebellion. They cannot put down the rebellion; it is too popular. They have to call on England for help. England sends a thousand troops over to quell this rebellion. That says something about the popularity and extent of it. And of course the rebellion is crushed.

And governments learn something from rebellions.

They learn that they must make some concessions, but not too many concessions. They learn they must prepare for harsher measures. They must try harder to keep people apart. So in the South, for instance, they use whites as slave patrols to go after fugitive black people, and they give whites certain little advantages, even though those whites are servants. Bacon's Rebellion is a lesson for people on all sides, but it's only one part of this long conflict between rich and poor in American history—before the Revolution, during the Revolution, after the Revolution.

This anger that existed between the rich and the poor before the Revolution shows itself in the midst of the Revolution. Because there is class division among soldiers, between officers and enlisted men. This is an old story in the military: there are the officers and there are the enlisted men, and it is very crass, because the officers in the Revolutionary Army are treated very well. They get good pay. They get resplendent uniforms. They eat well. The privates get very little pay to begin with, but their pay stops coming after the first year of the war. And when their enlistments are supposed to be up, they are not allowed to go home. And they're in rags, so they rebel.

Here's something that people don't learn when they

learn about the American Revolution. They don't learn that there were mutinies throughout the Revolution by the poor privates against the rich officers.

In 1781 there was a mutiny of over a thousand soldiers in what was called the Pennsylvania Line, who were fed up with the way they were treated. Faced with this, Washington worried that it would spread, and made concessions to them. Allowed a bunch of them to simply leave the army.

Later that month, there was a mutiny in the New Jersey Line. Well, whereas the Pennsylvania mutiny was a matter of a thousand soldiers, the one in New Jersey was only by several hundred. And here, Washington, instead of making concessions, decided that he would punish the mutineers—and he had several of them shot.

Shortly after the New Jersey mutiny, the Pennsylvanian mutineers rebelled again. This time twelve of them were singled out to be executed, and six of them were immediately executed by a firing squad of their own fellow soldiers. Of the six who were shot down, five died immediately. One was wounded, and then a fellow soldier was ordered to put him out of his misery. After that, another six soldiers were put to death.

Conflict among the classes manifested itself most dramatically in Shays' Rebellion, which took place in western Massachusetts in 1786, named after Captain Daniel Shays, who had fought in the Revolution. That was just three years after the signing of the peace with England. Poor farmers in western Massachusetts, many of them veterans, could not pay the high taxes levied on them by the Massachusetts legislature, which was dominated by rich merchants. As a result of nonpayment, their farms, their livestock, their land had been taken away from them. Auctioned off. They organized. Thousands of them surrounded the courthouses where these auctions were taking place.

They surrounded courthouses in five different cities in western Massachusetts—in Northampton, Amherst, Great Barrington, Springfield, and Hampshire—and they would not allow the courts to proceed with the auctions. This took place not only in Massachusetts, but also in South Carolina, Maryland, New Jersey, and Pennsylvania.

The full story of the rebellion of poor farmers throughout the colonies after the Revolution has not been told. It is important, because it's a sign of the fact that when these veterans came back after the war, they had been promised things. They'd been promised land. They remember the words of the Declaration of Independence, but now they find that they're struggling for survival against a small number of people who are in control of the government.

This class struggle is the backdrop to the framing of the Constitution in 1787. As they approach the Constitutional Convention, the Founding Fathers are very, very conscious of what they just saw in western Massachusetts and in other parts of the colonies. They saw the rising of the poor against the rich. And when they're framing the Constitution, they are keeping that in mind.

On the eve of the Constitutional Convention in Philadelphia in 1787, General Henry Knox writes to Washington and says (I am not using his exact words), "These people, because they fought in the Revolution, against England, think that they are entitled to an equal share of the wealth of this country." He is warning Washington. In fact, when you look at the debates around the ratification of the Constitution, and when you look at the Federalist Papers [a collection of eighty-five articles that James Madison and Alexander Hamilton and John Jay wrote for the New York newspapers to persuade people to vote for the Constitution] you see an argument for ratification on the basis of needing a strong central government in order to put down trouble—to deal with troublemakers.

Federalist Paper Number 10, which James Madison wrote, argues for the Constitution because the Constitution will create a representative government, which will make it harder for a rebellion to occur and will cover all of the thirteen colonies. And it will be able to deal with the kind of problems that they had recently faced. He writes about these problems, these grievances, and the rage for paper money, something that poor people wanted, the farmers wanted, so that they could pay off their debts more easily.

This is always a difficult thing for Americans to accept because we revere the Founding Fathers. These are wise and great brilliant men, admirable in so many ways, but the fact is that the Constitution was shaped in the shadow of Shays' Rebellion. The Constitution was shaped in the fear of trouble—of slave uprisings, of uprisings of the poor. They wanted to set up a strong federal government that would have an army that could control things, put down rebellions, and, as they said in another one of the Federalist Papers, filter the grievances of people through a body of legislators, the Senate, so that by the time the grievances made their way through the Senate, their bitterness would be softened.

The Senate would blow on the broth from the House of Representatives to cool down the hot passions steaming up from the people.

Right, exactly.

But the narrative you just laid out, of mutiny, class division, the alienation of American from American, not only doesn't fit with what we're taught (which I think is a thread that runs throughout your book), but it also doesn't perhaps recognize the real foment for self-government that was going on among regular people.

Not landowners or gentry, but people who caulked the side of ships, people who made rope, people who brewed beer in their houses, people who baked—they might have been dismissed a hundred years later by Karl Marx's idea of the petite bourgeoisie, but there was about a paper-thin difference between them and the fellow at the next bench who was their employee. There was a passion that also comes out of the writings and the stories that people tell of that time, for liberty, that is quite removed from this sort of dreary litany of oppression and oppressors that you have just given. Wasn't there?

Well, unquestionably. There were many, many people in the colonies who welcomed independence from England, and there were people who welcomed the Revolution. And in fact the Declaration of Independence was a very remarkable historical document that promised things that hadn't been promised before—an equal right to life, liberty, and the pursuit of happiness.

It was a very noble dream. There were people who fought for this dream, and there was something right about being independent from England, but at the same time, there is a part of the story that is left out.

The part you're describing—the rope makers and sailors who gathered in Boston and were put down in the Boston Massacre, the working people who gathered in 1773, and the Boston Tea Party—that is the part of the story we all learn about. We all learn about the Boston Massacre. We all learn about the Boston Tea Party. We learn about the Stamp Act. We learn about the heroism at Bunker Hill and at Valley Forge and so on.

But I have felt that there is an important part of the story left out: when England was removed from its control of the colonies, we did *not* then get democracy. We did *not* then get equality. Slavery still existed. In fact, slavery was written into the Constitution without even using the word. This was a slave owner's nation that was created despite the Declaration of Independence, and the nation that was created was dominated by the rich.

But we also didn't get serfdom. I mean, there were many other models extant at that point in 1776 or in 1789 when the Constitution was ratified. There was rule by aristocracy. There was rule by landowners. There were people who were tied to the land in an intergenerational way so that they couldn't move freely inside the boundaries of their own country. We didn't get those things either. Counter to the story you are telling, we got what might be seen as a self-correcting system. Once it recognizes or is forced to recognize its abuses, forced to confront its own internal contradictions, at some point it self-repairs. Now, maybe not always right away, maybe not always fast enough. But there is bottom-up as well as top-down communication, isn't there?

Well, you have it in a system of partial representation,

or inadequate representation. Remember, the Senate was not popularly elected, the president was not popularly elected, the House of Representatives was elected by people with property. Only one of the states, Pennsylvania, said that people without property could vote.

So yes, you had a certain degree of representation, but the self-correction that we very often pride ourselves on has never taken place in the arena of wealth versus poverty. At the time of the Revolution, probably 1 percent of the people in the colonies owned 40 percent of the wealth. If you look today at the figures of concentration of wealth in the United States, about 1 percent of the population owns about 40 percent of the wealth. My point is that there has been consistency throughout American history in the monopolization of wealth. Not total. Enough distributed below to create a middle class that would be content enough so that there wouldn't be rebellion.

Some correction, but not self-correction—in the sense that it hasn't been the leaders who corrected themselves. It was the people who organized, who created social movements, and who changed their own conditions, generally not through the organs of representative government but through direct action.

I'm talking now about economics and about the rights of working people. The conditions of working people, the wages, the hours of working people still now in this century remain a problem. That has not been self-correcting.

Because there is nothing in the Constitution that grants the right of a job, the right of social security, the right of health care, the right of housing—nothing. Working people have to do this by themselves. The system set up by the Founding Fathers did not take care of the problem of poverty and class division in this country.

What happened is that in the nineteenth century, working people began to organize, and they changed their condition through social struggle, through strikes and boycotts, through direct action. In that way, we *have* achieved some modicum of reform in this country. When you move from the economic situation to the situation of slavery, as you said, it took a long time for that correction to take place. To use the word *self-correction* gives too much credit to the people at the top, suggesting that, well, suddenly Lincoln was seized by a desire to free the slaves or Congress suddenly was won over to the idea of abolition.

It took a powerful social movement, the antislavery movement in this country, to put pressure on Lincoln before the Emancipation Proclamation, to put pressure on Congress before it passed the Thirteenth, Fourteenth, and Fifteenth Amendments. So I think it is a mistake to give young people going to school and learning history the idea that we have a wonderful mechanism here that's self-correcting when things go wrong.

It is not self-correcting. It is corrected when people organize on behalf of their own needs—on behalf of equality and justice, as black people have done throughout history, as working people have done, as women have done, as in recent years disabled people have done, or in recent years gay and lesbian people have done. Because the mechanism itself has not been self-correcting for them.

But to recoil from the term self-correcting *is also to say that we are not one people, that we are not one society, that we are not limbs of a common body, but that in fact we are multiple peoples at constant war or in constant struggle and opposition with one another.*

We *are* certainly in opposition with one another. Resources are scarce, and people are struggling for these scarce resources. Jobs are scarce, and people struggle against one another for jobs. Black people against white people. Men against women. More skilled against less skilled. Native-born against immigrants.

Conflicts have always existed among people, but I think it is also important to note that these conflicts have played into the hands of those who reap the greatest wealth in society, that they have benefited from the fact that white and black people have been at odds with one another. It has made it more difficult for people, all of whom have a certain common interest in their own difficult conditions, to unite. And, yes, this has been a constant problem in the history of the United States in bringing about fundamental social change.

So is that one of the threads that connects Columbus's conquest, the Pequot Massacre, Bacon's Rebellion, Shays' Rebellion, and the mutineers of the Revolutionary era? Is there a thread that runs through all of those events that should inform our understanding of the country and its history?

I think the thread that runs through all of those events is the conflict between the best ideals of the human race, the ideals expressed in the Declaration of Independence, and the reality that people have faced, with slavery, with racism, with economic exploitation, with sexual inequality. The conflict between the ideals and the reality, I think, has been the thread running through American history.

And if we bring these stories to the table, to be presented alongside the victorious generals on horseback, the wise Founding Fathers, and so on, how do we benefit in the twenty-first century from that broader portrait?

We benefit by recognizing that, if we're going to change society, we cannot depend on something created two hundred years ago by the Founding Fathers, and we cannot depend on the people in power. We cannot depend on the president and Congress and the Supreme Court. Looking at this long thread of struggle and looking at the way things have changed, we learn that it's up to us, as citizens. It makes us better citizens. It makes us active citizens, more than voters. It makes us people who day-to-day get together with other people. It really gives us a new idea of democracy.

Democracy does not come from the top. Democracy comes from ordinary people seeing what they have in common and seeing what they are lacking. When ordinary people get together, they put their energy together. They protest together, they demand things together, they form a movement—and that is how change takes place. That is how we can get closer and closer to the ideals of the Declaration of Independence.

So when we find out that someone like Equiano, in addition to shining a light on the evils of slavery, was someone who aspired to own slaves himself, that shouldn't negate the validity of his story, that shouldn't make us question his sincerity. What should we do when we find out that a pivotal person also had some real flaws?

You know, sometimes we find out that this person who was a great symphony conductor has a private life that is less than noble. And the question is: should we then not listen to his symphonies anymore?

People who do important and noble things very often turn out, on close inspection, to have all sorts of personal flaws or contradictions in their behavior. And this is something we shouldn't ignore, shouldn't hide, but at the same time, it shouldn't therefore cause us to say, well since this person isn't ideal, then we shouldn't listen to what this person has to say.

We have learned in recent years that Martin Luther King was not a perfect person in his personal life. But this is something that you might say all people have in common.

What all people have in common is flaws and contradictions. What they don't have in common is that some people are not admirable in their relationship to society. Some people are acquirers of wealth and makers of war. Other people, like King, struggle for justice and speak out against war. So, while there are certain things that all people have in common, there are other things that mark some as different. It's those differences that are crucial in assessing human beings. The differences are matters of morality and human rights and where people stand.

*   *   *

Andrew Jackson comes to us today on the $20 bill, but he also comes down to us in stories of being the great democratizer, the great populist, who opens up government to the common man. Is he that?

Andrew Jackson is an example of one of those people in American history who is deified. Anytime anybody draws up a list of great presidents, Andrew Jackson is pretty close to the top. I remember learning about him for the first time in school, how he opened the White House to the ordinary people and how he was a man of the people. And he brought democracy in some sense to the nation's capital, to the nation.

This is a very inadequate picture of Jackson because it omits his relationship to slavery, his relationship to the Indians, his attitude toward people who are not white, his land speculation, his personal enrichment, his role in the expulsion of the Indians from Georgia, Alabama, Mississippi, and Florida, and his broken promises to the Indians. Jackson himself is mostly lauded as a military hero. This is one of the problems with American history, that our military heroes somehow become the most important people in our history. Their military exploits are emphasized, but what they do in other parts of their lives is simply not paid attention to.

For instance, under Jackson antislavery literature was barred from the mail of the South. Now, mail everywhere in the country is controlled by the federal government, and therefore the states should not have had the power to bar antislavery literature from reaching the South. But the Southern states did that, and Jackson went along.

The federal government had jurisdiction over the disposal of Indian lands in the South. There was a statute to that effect. Andrew Jackson ignored that law and allowed the states to dispossess Indians in Georgia, Alabama, and Mississippi. He was a slaveholder himself, and he was a supporter of slavery. He was an Indian killer who enjoyed, as he himself said, participating in the killing of Indians. The picture of Jackson simply as a Democrat is not only bad in itself in distorting the picture of Jackson, but it is bad in that it gets us accustomed to sanitizing the pictures of our presidents, our leaders, gets us accustomed to ignoring what their relationship was to people who are oppressed.

The United States had at that time recently acquired Florida. Florida was still largely settled by Indian tribes. What was Jackson's role in bringing Florida into the rest of the United States?

There is an interesting story about Jackson's relationship to Florida, because Jackson was involved in fighting the Seminole Indians. The Seminoles were an Indian tribe who fought back against what was happening to them. Jackson fought against them for several years, and a lot of Seminoles were killed in the process. He commanded raids, crossing from the United States into Florida, which was Spanish territory, in order to go after the Seminoles. He did that so often and with such effect that the Spanish felt they couldn't continue to hold on to Florida. Jackson's military forays into Florida laid the basis for Spain agreeing to sell Florida to the United States.

On our maps it looks very nice. I remember the maps being shown to us as schoolkids showing westward expansion, and almost everything was either a purchase or a cession. It was all very benign.

There was a Florida Purchase. There was a Mexican Cession. There was the Louisiana Purchase. All of these euphemisms concealed the fact that these places were taken either by violence or by some kind of underhanded act, and that they were all forerunners of wars against the Indians, taking their territory from them.

The Florida Purchase was really the result of an aggressive war fought outside of U.S. territory by Andrew Jackson. Likewise, the Mexican Cession (as it is labeled on the map) was not simply a peaceful transfer of land but was the result of a bitter war between Mexico and the United States, from the years 1846 to 1848.

When the United States goes in and begins to try to pull up Indian culture by the roots in Florida, doesn't it also dislocate a growing Afro-Indian civilization, for want of a better term, Afro-Indian culture?

Yes, there was an interesting Afro-Indian culture in Florida—and to some extent in other parts of the South, but more in Florida than anywhere else. That is where Indians mingled with slaves, close relationships developed, and they produced offspring who were of mixed parentage. Taking Florida and turning it into part of the American slave territory disrupted that, yes.

Was Andrew Jackson someone who had ambitions to not only expand America westward but expand slave America westward?

There is no doubt about Jackson's interest in expanding slave territory westward. Texas was part of Mexico; some people forget that these days. And more and more white settlers moved into Mexican land. Jackson encouraged the movement of white people into Texas so that white people soon became a majority, making it possible for the United States later to annex Texas. That added a huge chunk of land for slave territory and for the growing of cotton in particular.

Was slavery part of the calculus involving Texas from the very beginning? Or was it an ancillary effect—one that was to some people's benefit but was just something they happened to get in the bargain?

I think there were multiple reasons for wanting Texas. One was the acquisition of more land. But I think slavery was a crucial element in the desire to acquire Texas, because it was known that, if Texas were acquired, it would be slave territory. So the motive in acquiring Texas was certainly very strongly the desire to extend slave territory.

* * *

One part of the American story that doesn't get told a lot is how often people fought back. You mentioned the Seminoles. Occasionally Indian tribes put up ferocious resistance. Why should we recall Tecumseh?

Starting roughly around 1811 and going on for another decade or so, Tecumseh tried to rally several Indian tribes to unite against whites who were taking Indian land. Tecumseh is important not just for his role as a leader, but because he left in the record speeches that he made in which he explained why he was fighting against the white man. He thought the Indians had treated the white man properly when the white man arrived. But they had then been deceived, the treaties had been broken, and lands promised to them had been taken away from them. He deplored the fact that the white man was introducing into this continent the greed that accompanied the desire for land at the expense of others—land that would be owned privately—while he thought, according to Indian culture, that people should own land collectively.

So Tecumseh was not just an organizer of Indian people but was a spokesman for the idea that a spirit that Indian culture represented was being destroyed by what was happening.

Was there by this time, when the westward movement was already pretty well advanced, a sense among Indians that they were all Indians, whereas when the Europeans arrived they might have been five hundred separate countries—different languages, different cultures, different ideas about the world and about themselves—that they were now all Indians and had to put up a resistance that was different, because unless they fought back it was game over?

There's nothing like being attacked to create a practical need for unity among people who earlier had fought among themselves. The constant movement of white people into the West and the taking of more land certainly created more of an incentive for Indians to work together.

This did not work perfectly. The white settlers, the people who were organizing the white movement into Indian lands, very often played Indians against one another. They played the leaders of Indian tribes against the members of the tribe, by signing treaties with the leaders over the heads of the members. They used Indians to fight other Indians, and to betray other Indians. You know this is a very common feature of colonialism, of controlling other people—that is, to use people against one another, to divide them against one another.

What did the frontier look like in the 1860s and 1870s, and how does that line up against the image that we get of that time today through stories and books?

The image of the frontier is the image of cowboys and Indians, of courageous Americans moving west in their covered wagons and being attacked by Indians. There is no attention paid to the fact that these Americans in their covered wagons—although admittedly they were brave, remarkable people, hardy and courageous people—were moving into other people's land.

The image of benign Americans being attacked by Indians, the cowboy-and-Indian story, doesn't give an accurate picture because, from the Indian point of view, alien people were moving into land that the Indians had been hunting on and living on for centuries. And taking that land from them. And attacking them with great military force when they resisted.

You have already discussed the Sand Creek Massacre. How does the Sand Creek Massacre fit in with the sense that Americans had at the time, that they were eventually going to have a country that ran from sea to shining sea?

The movement into the West was understood by the people who were engaging in it as part of the march of a civilized country, from the Atlantic to the Pacific, while removing people who did not understand what civilization was—vicious heathen who had to be removed in order for progress to go forward. That was the motive of American expansion throughout the nineteenth century, until finally in 1890, in a semi-official way, the frontier was declared closed.

This was also the year of the massacre at Wounded Knee, South Dakota, where in a repetition of what had happened at Sand Creek in Colorado, American soldiers fell upon a peaceful Indian village and slaughtered people. So 1890 is an important turning point.

Is there a growing sense during any of this time, in the years after the Civil War, that the United States either as the several states or as the federal government is going to have to come up with a different answer to the future of native people in the country?

There was no real opposition in the United States to westward expansion. There were individuals and small groups that protested. There was literature. There was a woman named Helen Hunt Jackson, who wrote a book that was widely read, which was an account of the cruelties that were inflicted upon the Indians in the course of westward expansion.

So you might say there was a small part of the American public that was conscious of what was happening to the Indians, in the same way that a small part of the American public was conscious in the 1830s and 1840s of what was happening to black people.

But it wasn't a significant number of Americans, not significant enough to have any serious effect. The only effect it had was a search for reforms, and by reforms I mean the attempt that was made to put Indians on reservations and to send the young Indians to American schools, where they would be weaned away from tribal culture and become assimilated into the national culture. There was also a very concerted attempt to teach the Indians the value of personal acquisitiveness, as against the idea of collective ownership of property and sharing that had been part of Indian culture.

After the violence was over, let's say by 1890, and the land had been conquered by white men, then they could afford to look for ways to ease the situation by trying to assimilate the Indians and to Americanize them, you might say.

For a long time, there was no way that Indians could rise up out of this situation. It really isn't until the 1960s that Indians begin to organize and begin to study the history and begin to demand that their culture be recognized.

In A People's History, *you quote a newspaper of the 1840s: "The universal Yankee nation can regenerate and disenthrall the people of Mexico in a few years and we believe it is a part of our destiny to civilize that beautiful country." What is Manifest Destiny?*

The term *Manifest Destiny* was first used by a newspaper editor named John L. O'Sullivan. He said, "Providence has ordained for us the requirement of taking over this land and civilizing the people who stand in the way of our expansion." The phrase *Manifest Destiny* came to represent the idea that it is the mission of the United States to move into other territories and to civilize other people. Mexicans were looked upon as uncivilized, as not deserving their own independence. The idea of Manifest Destiny soon became applied to the whole idea of

American expansion, not just southward into Mexico, but also westward into California and Oregon.

Later on, when continental expansion had partly reached its limits, when we were at the Pacific Ocean and at the Rio Grande, that idea of Manifest Destiny was applied to moves overseas.

The idea of civilizing other people has remained a constant in relation to Latin America and in relation to people in other parts of the world. When the United States was confronted in 1898, 1899, with a prospect of taking the Philippines from Spain, President McKinley said we must do it in order to Christianize and civilize the Filipinos.

So you had in the 1840s a general call in the press and among politicians for the idea of moving southward into Mexican territory—and also westward, because the Mexicans at that time owned what is now California, Nevada, New Mexico, and Arizona—and to do this in the guise of civilizing these people. Of course, the real reason was extending slave territory.

This was understood by the antislavery people in the United States, for instance by Henry David Thoreau, who was part of the antislavery movement of New England.

Thoreau spent that famous night in prison in Massachusetts because he had refused to pay taxes in protest against the war in Mexico, which he saw as a conspiracy on the part of the slave owners and the American government to extend slavery into other territory.

And in fact when the United States did win the Mexican War, in 1848, it took over 40 percent of Mexican territory, very rich and important land that is now the U.S. Southwest.

It's ironic that today there are people in Arizona and California who are erecting walls and setting up posses to prevent Mexicans from coming northward into territory that once was part of Mexico. At the time of the Mexican War, most people in the country were not really aware of what was happening. They were not aware that President Polk had written in his diary, even before the war started, that he coveted California and was looking for a way to acquire it.

What most people knew was that there had been a clash of soldiers on the border between Texas and Mexico. There was disputed territory between the Rio Grande and the Nueces River; American and Mexican patrols had clashed there, and American soldiers had been killed. Immediately

Polk announced that we must go to war because, as he put it, American blood had been shed on American soil.

It was not quite American soil, it was disputed territory, but it was that kind of deception that has led to so many wars. So many wars have started with incidents, often fabricated or exaggerated. We had such incidents at the beginning of the Philippine War, and we had one in the Gulf of Tonkin in 1964. The incident on the border between Texas and Mexico was an opportunity for Polk to do what he had wanted to do all along, to acquire all of that land that Mexico owned.

But as the war went on, the antislavery movement began to have an effect. More and more people began to question the Mexican War. Abraham Lincoln, a young congressman from Illinois, got up in Congress and introduced what were called the Spot Resolutions, which demanded to know from the president where this spot was where American blood had been shed on American soil.

So there were more and more congressmen who questioned the war. And there were soldiers who questioned the war. Many of them were immigrants, Irish immigrants, who had no prospects in life and who joined the army on the promise of some pay and some recognition.

As the war went on, as the mayhem of the war grew more bitter, with bloody battles and the deaths of soldiers mounting, more and more American soldiers deserted. In fact, near the end of the war, as General Winfield Scott was marching toward Mexico City, he woke up one morning and half of his regiments were gone. I remember one specific instance when Massachusetts volunteers back from the war came to a dinner that had been organized to honor their commander, and when the commander got up to speak, they booed and hissed because they had lost half their men in the war. And they were not sure why in the world they were fighting.

As they marched into Mexican towns, and as they participated in and watched ugly incidents that took place, a number of Americans deserted to the Mexican side, especially Irish soldiers, immigrants from Ireland who didn't know what they were getting into when they joined up and who now had seen enough of bloodshed. They formed a battalion to fight against their own countrymen, the Batallón de San Patricio. Or, as they called it, the Saint Patrick's Battalion.

Eventually many of them were caught and tried by the army, and some of them were executed. But to this day the

Mexicans celebrate the San Patricio Battalion. Every year there is a ceremony in Mexico City to honor its members.

* * *

How often was Manifest Destiny intertwined with religion as part of its appeal, as part of its advocacy for an American subduing of the entire North American continent?

That idea of Providence giving us the right to go into other people's land—that idea is a persistent one throughout American history. In fact, it starts with the Puritans. It starts with the religious people of New England. It starts with Cotton Mather the minister, the theologian, giving his blessing to the massacre of Indians on the grounds that they are not Christians and that Providence has given us the right to do what we want to these heathens. God and religion appear again and again in the writings of the early settlers of New England and of the first governor of Massachusetts, John Winthrop, who talks about the city on a hill and how God is on the side of the settlers.

God is always on the side of the people who fight in a war, and it's always assumed that God has nothing to do with the other side. This becomes especially persuasive when the other side consists of people who don't seem to believe in the same God that we do.

In your view, how should what we have just been talking about alter, reshape, or shade our national mythology? The Indian massacres, the westward expansion, the war against Mexico—how should these things shape what we think of as that time in our national life? How should that intrude on our national mythology?

I think a new, refreshed view of American history might help this country enormously, by introducing the idea that the United States is not the savior of the world. We are not the bringer of democracy, of civilization, to other countries. It would be a sobering self-examination, and a recognition on the part of the American people that we are not special. We are not endowed by Providence with some special rights over other people. We are a people like other peoples. And we should stop requiring that our country be a superpower.

We are inevitably a superpower in certain respects. We are enormously wealthy, and we have made certain obvious technological progress. But that should not create the idea that we therefore have a right to control countries, to send troops into other countries, to send warships into other seas, to decide for ourselves what governments other countries should have.

An individual who has built himself or herself up in life, that person in gaining great wealth perhaps has developed a picture of himself as a really important person, and somehow transfers the advantage of wealth into a moral advantage—that is, assumes that great wealth confirms great goodness. At a certain point, a person like that has to come to a recognition that, well, I'm a human being like others. I don't deserve more privilege than others. I don't deserve to try to control other people's lives.

In other words, we have to start thinking of America as one among many, as a nation of people equal to other peoples but not superior to them. What that would do, aside from being an enormous psychological change for Americans, would be to bring about an honest recognition of who we are and what our limitations are—without denigrating ourselves, without demeaning ourselves. That would change the policies of our country if enough citizens recognize that. We don't need our ships on every sea. We have enormous wealth; we can use it for good purposes. We can use it for people here at home to make our lives better. We can use it to help people who are in trouble, and people who are the victims of earthquakes and hurricanes, or starvation, or famine.

Why would we have that kind of national inward look, when—if we look back over the last hundred years—the country has become stable, powerful, rich in most places on most days, well governed, and likely to protect the rights of the individual. What is going to set off an orgy of national self-examination if things in the end look like they've gone pretty well?

It depends on who's looking. For many Americans, it looks as if it has gone pretty well. We are a very rich and prosperous country. We are a country with enormous wealth. We have 40 million people without health insurance. We have 2 million people in prison; we have one of the highest rates of incarceration in the world. This is a sign of a kind of sickness.

There must be something wrong when we have people all over the country living in ways that create desperation, that create a demand for drugs.

We are not number one in the world in taking care of the needs of our people. We are, among industrial nations, almost last in the world in our record on infant mortality. The World Health Organization ranks us at about number twenty-five among nations in terms of decent and equitable health programs. There are many countries, even countries that are less developed than ours, that have higher rates of literacy than we do. I think it's important, if we're not going to become complacent, if we are not to head into trouble, that we begin to recognize the other side of our society.

You note that military forays into adjoining territory and other parts of the world have often been explained to the American people by a threat against our safety, our security, and our prosperity.

Would the kind of shift that you're suggesting in the way the people of this country think about themselves make it less likely that people elsewhere would threaten us?—using as an example the current threat of terrorist attacks against the United States.

This phenomenon of terrorism is very interesting, because it looks like a unique situation. People often say

9/11 changed everything or was a kind of experience that the United States has never had.

Of course, what happened on September 11, 2001, was unique in the way that all historical events are unique.

On the other hand, this phenomenon of fear, which then becomes a justification for aggressive action against another people or another nation—this is something that we have seen again and again. In fact, there was great fear of the Indians and fear of Indian massacres.

Now the difference between that situation and the present situation is that it was almost impossible to eliminate the clash of two peoples fighting for the same territory. In the case of the United States engaging in wars overseas in order to eliminate the fear of terrorism, this is not an inevitable clash. This is something that can be averted, I think, by very intelligent consideration of where terrorism comes from and what the best remedy is to deal with it.

All of our military action in the Middle East has not stopped terrorism but only inflames people who might become terrorists. The only defense against terrorism is to do something about its roots. And the roots of terrorism, whether we like to acknowledge it or not, are grievances.

Terrorists are reacting to their grievances in an immoral and fanatic way, but the grievances themselves may be genuine, and they may be felt not only by the terrorists, but by millions and millions of other people.

If the grievances have some legitimacy to them, then it is our responsibility to address these grievances: to think about withdrawing troops from the Middle East, to think about playing a different role on the question of Israel and Palestine.

Just as we have a right to be free from terrorists from the Middle East, the people of the Middle East have a right to be free from a different kind of terrorism—war. War is terrorism. I say this as a former bombardier in the Air Force, who dropped bombs on other people. Bombs terrorize people. They kill people, and they terrorize them. War is terrorism on a very large scale.

In fact, the wars waged by governments are at a level of terrorism far greater than that of any small body like Al Qaeda or the IRA or Palestinian suicide bombers. It's on a far greater scale than they are capable of. We need to define terrorism in such a way as to see other people as equal to ourselves. So yes, a different view of our history and our policies would make us safer.

Does every generation make these choices from scratch, from square one, or is there a way that the past reaches up, grabs us by the collar, and makes a claim on the present, makes a claim on the future?

The past is important; we don't start from scratch. Governments don't start from scratch. Business interests don't start from scratch. They start from a long history, and they become accustomed to certain ways of being in the world. Governments that are expansionist become accustomed to expansion. Businesses that make great profits become accustomed to these profits, so they inherit a certain way of thinking and being in the world. Then on the part of the citizenry, the people, there is a history of social movements. There is a history in this country of black people, of women, of people who struggle against war. There is a history of what they have done in the past, very often failing and sometimes succeeding. We all have that heritage to draw upon, and our challenge is to draw upon it in a way that's most constructive in fashioning a decent society.

PART II

"They Rebelled":
The Long Nineteenth Century

If you look at the history of the Lowell mills and the strikes that periodically racked the mill towns of Massachusetts, what do they teach you about the industrial revolution?

One of the things they do is to make you aware that the industrial revolution started before the Civil War.

The general impression is that up to the Civil War we were simply an agrarian society, and after the Civil War we became an industrial society. But industry came to New England in the 1820s. It came as soon as the power loom was invented and they could weave cotton to cloth mechanically. Then the textile mills grew in towns like Lowell and Lawrence, and places in Rhode Island.

Their workers were mostly girls. Girls would go into these mills at the age of twelve, and many of them would die by the age of twenty-five; they were working very, very hard. They were working long hours—twelve, fourteen, sixteen hours a day, six or seven days a week. They were getting up in the dark and going home in the dark, getting a half hour for lunch. They were struggling just to stay alive.

They had come to the mill because they had families back on the farm. These were farm girls coming into the city because it was becoming a cash economy. Money was entering the lives of these people, and now these girls were going to bring in some money.

Of course, they were going to bring very *little* money into the house, because they were getting something like 35¢ a day. It was these conditions that caused these girls, young women, to rebel. They formed associations. They put out a newspaper. And yes, starting in the 1820s and 1830s, they began going on strike. That alarmed not only the mill owners, but also some of the newspapers, which reported that these girls were *holding meetings* and, you know, this was not the proper thing for girls to do. They should know better and take their dutiful place in the industrial world.

But some wonderful literature came out of that struggle. One of these girls, Harriet Robinson, later recalled her first strike. She told how she talked to the other girls on her floor about the fact that elsewhere, in other mills, the girls would be going on strike, because they were fed up with how little they were getting and how hard they were working and the terrible conditions. And breathing in cotton fibers—you can imagine what that does to the lungs.

She was asking, "Will you go out on strike? Will you walk out?" The phrase used was "turn out." "Will you turn out?" And then when the moment came when the workers at other mills were turning out, she looked at her fellow workers and asked, "Well, are we going?"

Nobody moved.

Then she said, "Well, I'm going to move." And she did. And then the rest followed.

Later she said, "You know, I still look back on that as one of the great moments of my life."

The mill owners certainly began this process thinking that a working population of women was going to be more pliable, more easily dominated and controlled than a working population of men. But didn't they also respond with a certain paternalism to the desires of the women? There were choral societies, the newspaper you mention, sewing circles, schools begun inside the mill working units. Were these initiatives an attempt to make these women's lives more bearable so that they wouldn't rebel?

It is true that the owners tried to create a kind of social life for the girls outside the factory, even though they had very little time to engage in any of these things. But they tried. They did try to make it more palatable for them.

This has been a constant issue in the world of the factory. Does it come from a cynical attempt to keep people in line? Is there a grain of humanity in the owners that says, "Oh, we ought to do something for these people"?

There is a long tradition, into the twentieth century, of people like Henry Ford, thinking that he'll try to make life on the assembly line a little better. But it's never enough for workers, and certainly not for these young girls. No, it wasn't enough, and that is why they rebelled.

Do we see here the roots of what would later become the suffrage movement in a mass sense? Do we see here roots of women's consciousness as a political force?

Well, this was a period in which women came into the political conflicts of the day. While we can't find a specific organic connection between the strikes at the Lowell mills and the rise of women activists in the antislavery movement and in the feminist movement, there was a very close connection among women coming out as abolitionists and then coming out for the equality of women. In fact, you might say it became easier for women to begin to demand rights for themselves after they had established a kind of dignity for themselves by joining the abolitionist movement.

They were not totally welcomed in the antislavery movement. That is, these men who were opposed to slavery had still not begun to recognize the rights of women. So when there was an antislavery congress in London, the women had to sit in the balcony. But that inspired them, when they came back to the United States, to say, "No, we are not going to put up with this," and then they began to organize on their own.

That was the root of the women's movement—at the Seneca Falls Convention, where the women drew up a declaration of rights by rewriting the Declaration of

Independence to include women. "All men and women are created equal." Then they listed, as the Declaration of Independence had listed the grievances against the king of England, their grievances against men.

*   *   *

What was Gabriel's Rebellion, and where does this fall in the long line of slave revolts?

Gabriel is the first name of Gabriel Prosser, but there is a preference to call it Gabriel's Rebellion, because Prosser was the slave owner's name. It came in the early 1800s with a thousand black people trying to ignite a larger rebellion. It failed, as all U.S. slave rebellions did before the Civil War. But they at least were a manifestation of the refusal of slaves to accept their condition. Slave rebellions go back to the seventeenth century, almost as soon as slavery was introduced into the colonies, with the first black people coming to Jamestown in 1619.

The most important one was Nat Turner's Rebellion of 1831, in Virginia, a very powerful, organized attempt on the part of thousands of black people to take over plantations, to invade plantation territory. It was violent—they killed owners, and they went on a rampage. They were put down, and a number of them, including Nat Turner, were executed.

The rebellion was a kind of signal to the South that this might happen again, and on a larger scale. It made the South determined to put down any sign of rebellion, and to make sure, for instance, that abolitionist literature was not spread in the South.

The 1830s saw the beginning of an abolitionist movement in the country, starting in New England. William Lloyd Garrison put out his abolitionist newspaper, *The Liberator*, and Frederick Douglass, a former slave, put out his own newspaper, *The North Star*. Abolitionist and antislavery tracts began to spread throughout the country, but the South was determined not to let this sentiment spread.

It's interesting that you mentioned that all of them failed. They were put down, often in very purposely cruel and public ways, to demonstrate the cost of this kind of rebellion. If they were all put down, in short periods of time the ringleaders caught and rounded up, with people telling on each other in court proceedings, why were these revolts so threatening to the South? If whites had all the power, all the guns, all the state power, all the blood-hounds, why were the slave revolts able to send an electric jolt into the population of the South?

Rebellions always suggest to the people in power a possibility that one day they might succeed. We are very often surprised at the extent of force that is employed by people in authority against signs of rebellion, when we see how these rebellions fail. But people in power seem to have a kind of foresight. That is, they understand that tiny acts of protest can easily turn into larger acts of protest. And the idea of the people in power is to stifle them with such overwhelming power as to discourage future rebellion.

It happens in our time. You have seven people on a picket line, and they look around, and there are fifty policemen in riot gear who've been sent out to deal with them. They wonder, *What are they afraid of? What are they worried about?*

And I think the answer is that, yes, the people in power may have a clearer idea than the people on the picket line of what the possibilities are for small acts of protest to turn into large acts of rebellion. In fact, they're right, for the history of social movements is a history of small groups of people starting out apparently powerless, easily controlled, easily put down, and yet they rise again. And again and again they become larger and larger, and before you know it, you have a movement. An important movement.

The suppression of slave revolts in the South had to be done and had to be done decisively, yet it did not resolve the situation. The resentment of people against their condition may be kept under control for a while, and the people who are being oppressed may then themselves hold back, even appear to be content with their condition. But under the surface they're brimming with indignation—and waiting for the moment. Of course, for slaves the moment came when the Civil War gave them an opportunity finally to run away, to escape from the plantations.

Going back to the period before the Civil War, apart from these sudden eruptions, these spasms of violence in slave uprisings, did black resistance take more day-to-day, everyday forms?

Yes, I think that is important to recognize, because if you look only at the rebellions, which were sporadic and you might say occasional, you might conclude that most slaves just accepted their situation. There were many, many forms of slave resistance that were not as dramatic as rebellion. There was feigning illness and not doing their work the way they were supposed to. But probably the biggest form of slave resistance was running away.

That's what the Underground Railroad was about. There were huge numbers of slaves who wanted to run away but didn't have the capacity to do it. Harriet Tubman and other people went south to help slaves run away, to give them the possibility of doing that.

The high point of slave resistance before the Civil War came when slaves ran away and then had to deal with the Fugitive Slave Act of 1850. The Fugitive Slave Act gave the federal government the responsibility of returning slaves to their masters. Federal officials would get twice as much money if a slave was sent back to slavery than if he or she was declared free. In response, abolitionists organized themselves into what they called vigilante groups, which has a different connotation than what we think of today as vigilantes.

The idea of vigilante groups was that they would be vigilant—on the lookout for escaped slaves. If these escapees were apprehended by the federal government, then these abolitionist groups would rescue them.

A number of very dramatic rescues took place in the 1850s. Abolitionists, white and black, would break into police stations and courthouses to rescue slaves, then send them on their way to Canada.

By the 1850s, after twenty years of antislavery agitation, there had been a change of opinion in the North about slavery. When juries were faced with the problem of acquitting or convicting those white and black people who had helped slaves to escape, who had violated the Fugitive Slave Act, who had broken into courthouses and so on, often these juries voted to acquit them.

William Lloyd Garrison, Wendell Phillips, Frederick Douglass, and others started out being the objects of ridicule and anger by their white neighbors in the North, but things changed. By the 1850s, important people in the North were speaking out against slavery.

Amid this ferment of jailbreaks and runaways, there was a serious reconsideration and reexamination of slavery going on. People began to question whether it made economic sense for the South to continue to retain slavery as an institution. Looking back from the twenty-first century, did slavery make a big economic impact in the South? Did it make sense for the South? Did it help the economy of the nation as a whole?

Well, we have to consider that cotton had become a very, very important commodity—not just for the South, which grew it, but also for the North, which turned it into cloth, as well as the merchants who exported and sold it. The South and its economy were important to the nation.

There were now 4 million black slaves, and you can measure the growth of slavery along with the growth of cotton growing in the South. Slavery became absolutely essential to the plantation system in the South. Now, there has been argument among historians as to whether the economics of slavery made sense, whether the Southern slave owners would have been better off with free labor. It's possible that the South would have been better off freeing the slaves under the conditions that developed after the Civil War—black people "free" but still half enslaved.

The question is whether that would have been the rational thing for slave owners to do, and thus avoid civil war. But I think there is always a psychological element that enters into it. Whether slavery was profitable or not didn't matter, because the psychology of a slave-owning aristocracy was such that the life of plantation owners was built around a slave plantation.

Slavery gave them wealth and a life of great privilege and superiority in which they could enjoy all the finer things. They didn't want to disrupt it. I think that psychological factor, that cultural factor, may have been as important as economic considerations in the retention of slavery.

A nineteenth-century writer named George Fitzhugh wrote a bestseller called Cannibals All *that suggests that the workers of the new factories of the North were every bit as much enslaved as people tied to the land and picking cotton, black people in the South. That caused a sensation. Was it common among workers on both sides of the Mason-Dixon Line to see parallels in their condition?*

George Fitzhugh's argument was very compelling. It was a sophisticated and clever defense of slavery, saying, "You know, it's not simply that we have slaves and you have free people. We just have different forms of slavery." In a limited sense, you might say that Fitzhugh was a Marxist before there were Marxists, in that he saw the worker of the North, the proletariat of the North, as a slave to the industrial giants of the North. And he pointed to the hypocrisy of the North, which was railing against slavery while maintaining wage slavery. Although we don't know how many people or what percentage of people in the North and South, there were some who responded to this argument.

You point out in your book that one thousand families in the South controlled about the same amount of wealth as the other almost seven hundred thousand families who were counted in the 1850 census. Why did the white working class go to war to defend, to preserve that system?

Of course, you might ask that question in any war, because in any war it's the working people who go to war on behalf of a system that doesn't offer any great promise of living a better life. But it's certainly true that the South was an extreme example of this.

I suppose one answer is that it seems it's not that hard to persuade young people to go to war if you can present them with a cause—if you can show them that they're fighting for a principle, for a way of life. If you can locate an enemy for them to hate. And it wasn't hard to hate the North, which had, you might say, precipitated this war, by refusing to accept the secession of the Southern states and which looked upon the South as uncivilized because it had slavery. In other words, a working class can be propagandized into a war that is against its interests, and that certainly took place in the South.

Then, of course, there is also the race question and the fact that white people could be told that, if they didn't fight this war, black people would rise up and take over the South—that they were fighting to maintain the position of white supremacy over these 4 million black people.

But then you have to understand that all of this did not work well after a while. That is, white soldiers in the Confederacy, especially as the bloodiness of that war became extreme, especially as the war went on and on and men were dying on the battlefield in huge numbers—these young white kids began to question the war.

Huge desertions began to take place from the Confederate Army. This is a story that is not very well known. In the minds of most Americans who go to school and study the Civil War, the Confederacy appears as a kind of solid, loyal block.

But it wasn't.

There were desertions of the soldiers, and then there were rebellions of the soldiers' families back home. There were women in Georgia whose husbands were fighting—some of whose husbands had died—and by 1863 and 1864 these women were rioting against the slave owners, pointing out that the plantation owners were growing cotton instead of food. Cotton was profitable; food was not. They were starving while their men were giving their lives.

So there was a lot of disloyalty in the Confederacy. Conscription had to be introduced; they had to draft people into the army.

War had changed a lot during the nineteenth century. We were now in a time when armies stayed in the field the whole year round. That was a big departure from the days when people used to go home and plant and harvest, and then fight. Taking an agrarian population away from their farms for the entire year almost guaranteed there was going to be hunger and privation in the South.

Yes. And of course the Civil War also introduced new, deadlier weapons. Six hundred thousand men died in the battles of the Civil War—in a population of about 30 or 35 million people. That would be equivalent today to 4 or 5 million dead in a war. There were grisly scenes on the battlefield, and you know they didn't have the medical facilities that we have today when so many people are wounded but stay alive. Huge numbers of amputations took place right there in the field without anesthetics. It's not surprising that there was rebellion in the Confederacy.

Class conflict in the Civil War is too often unrecognized in the histories of the period, which very often dwell on the battles, and which present the Civil War as "the North versus the South." Well, it was not just the North versus the South. It was also the North versus the North and the South versus the South. It was the rich against the poor. It was the draft rioters, not just in New York but also in other cities, noting that the rich were getting out of serving by paying $300.

By the way, the same thing was true in the South. The rich could get out of conscription by paying sums of money.

One of the turning points in the Civil War, by common agreement, is the entry of freedmen and runaway slaves into the ranks of the Union Army. How did that change the war?

Close to two hundred thousand ex-slaves fought in the Civil War. They had not been welcome at first, but the Northern army became desperate for men as the war went on. In the view of many historians—certainly the great black historian W.E.B. DuBois made this point, that black soldiers made a crucial difference in the victory of the North over the South. Besides their contributions to the army, they made a crucial difference in bringing about a change in the Northern political structure's willingness to change the Constitution, to adopt the Thirteenth, Fourteenth, and Fifteenth Amendments. They were an important force in the country now, not just militarily but also politically.

But weren't we also sort of trapped in a paradoxical situation, where there was rising resentment toward black people because there was perception of the war as being fought for them, and over them, at the same time as there were forces inside the policy-making apparatus, the opinion-making apparatus of the United States, that didn't want black soldiers to enter the Union ranks?

That's right. That's why it took a while before they were allowed to enter. But military desperation drove the government to enlist them. Then they came back from the military, as has often been true in America's wars, demanding their rights, demanding change. And I think that this had an effect on Congress, and on the North in general, although the North remained racist.

You talk about the change in the character of the war due to the fact that black people were fighting for their own freedom, with ensuing changes in popular opinion in the North, but didn't this also send an electric charge through the people of the South, that black people were now fighting in the army? This was not an unnoticed development.

Certainly. It was frightening to Southerners that black people who had been slaves were now fighting against them. When black prisoners were taken by the Confederate Army, they were very often shot.

So they were not treated as soldiers.

No, because the idea of them being treated as ordinary

soldiers was repugnant to the people in the Southern armies.

* * *

Let's jump ahead to the end of the war and the creation of the Freedmen's Bureau. As you noted, there was some growing sentiment that, now that the war was over, there should be some addressing of black aspiration.

The Freedmen's Bureau was created to help black people in the transition from slavery to freedom. And for a while it offered promise, but ultimately it was unsuccessful because it could not give the freed slaves what they really needed, which was land of their own. The Freedmen's Bureau could give them schools, could bring educators down into the South, but black people were trapped economically—trapped very often on the plantations where they had been slaves. Because they did not have land of their own, in order to survive they had to go back to work for the plantation owner as tenant farmers.

They were held in semi-slavery. The Southern states adopted Black Codes, as they were called, which restricted the lives of these tenant farmers almost in the way that slavery had restricted them.

Didn't the divisions in the North all during the Civil War manifest themselves now with the Freedmen's Bureau? Some of the people running that and related bureaus had just been in uniform fighting against the South, and some of them were seized by a zeal to remake the country with a new dispensation under which black people could be free.

How did they lose? What happened? Was there a shift—a sudden shift underneath their feet that made it impossible to move on with land redistribution, that made it impossible legally to continue giving farms and land to black farmers?

Well, the most important thing that happened was a brief period of entry into political life by black people. Protected by federal troops in the South, who had been sent to enforce the Fourteenth and Fifteenth Amendments, for several years, black people were actually voted into state legislatures—and in South Carolina, there actually was a black majority in the state's House of Representatives.

There was a really quite remarkable period of what was called Radical Reconstruction. But it was not useful to the political leaders of the North, they realized after a while, to give all this political power to black people—and at the expense of their relationships with the old planter class of the South.

They wanted a national economic system. They wanted railroads both North and South. They wanted banks in the North to be able to have relations with Southern plantation owners. Those economic ties became more important to them than doing something for the ex-slaves.

It was that recognition of the common economic interest of the Northern elite with the Southern elite that led to the removal of federal troops from the South. In a sense, they were saying to the white South, "Okay now, we're giving the South back to you, and the fate of black people now rests in your hands."

In the early parts of the war, Lincoln insisted this was not a war to free the slaves but to save the Union, but clearly by the later stages of the war, ending slavery had become part of the North's program by common consent. Are you saying that, once the war was over and Reconstruction was being reconsidered, the economic interests trumped these other political concerns, and human rights concerns?

Yes. I think the economic interests were paramount.

After all, human rights concerns in general have not been primary for the people who run the economic system, the social system. Human rights are recognized only when they are useful.

For that brief period after the Civil War, when it was useful for the political leaders of the North to give the vote to black people and therefore give the North political control, that was fine. You might say the voting rights of black people were useful in electing a Republican president. Grant was elected by the margin of black voters in the South after the Civil War. But that interest faded, and the economic interest that we're talking about became paramount.

There was a very close election in 1876, and the Democrats won the popular vote, but there was a dispute about electoral votes in a number of states. Even though the Democratic candidate, Samuel Tilden, had won two hundred thousand more votes and should have been president by popular vote, the disputed electoral votes prevented that outcome.

A kind of arrangement was made, a compromise. The Republicans and the Democrats said, "Okay, we'll let Hayes—the Republican, with fewer votes—become president, but in return Hayes will remove the federal troops from the South."

This was the turning point, the signal that the black person was no longer useful to Northern economic and political interests. There then began, from the 1870s on into the twentieth century, the worst possible period for black people in the South after the Civil War.

So in your view, leaving the black people of the South to their fate completes a process that takes them from slavery without submission to emancipation without freedom?

Yes, exactly. You have moments in that period that dramatized the change.

I'm thinking of the year 1868, when a black minister named Henry Turner, who had been elected to the Georgia legislature with the support of black Georgians, faced expulsion under the threat of violence. His very eloquent speech in reply has been recorded in history.

One of the things that happened during Reconstruction is that black people, once removed from slavery, got a glimpse of their possibilities. We saw it earlier in Frederick Douglass and now we see it in Henry Turner. He speaks to the South as he says, "I am not going to let you take away my manhood." But of course they expelled him. Many years later, in the 1960s during the Vietnam War, the Georgia legislature expelled Julian Bond because he spoke out against the Vietnam War.

*   *   *

Is there a thread, almost a DNA relationship, that ties together runaway slaves and striking Lowell mill girls and Southern bread rioters and skedaddling Confederate soldiers and workers in the Freedmen's Bureau—that ties them together in a history of nineteenth-century America?

I think the thing that ties them together is the persistent refusal of people to stay in a state of subjection. In spite of the enormous power of slave owners, of mill owners, of the government, the insistence of apparently power-less people that they will not accept their condition is a current that runs through American history. And it's too often unrecognized, as we tell American history from the standpoint of the people in power, the presidents and the congressmen and the Supreme Court and the industrial-ists and the so-called important people in society.

I think it's important to pull all of that together and rec-ognize it, because if we don't, we're losing the possibility of inspiring ourselves to join in whatever movement and resistance there is in our time.

When I read your book, the Civil War ends up being sort of a massive exclamation point stuck into the middle of the nineteenth century. But I don't know whether to conclude that it's a cataclysm that sets a lot of things free and into motion, or whether it's the beginning of a reconsolidation by the powerful people in society whom you were just talking about.

I think the Civil War is both. It's a consolidation of power, the joining of the North and South in saving a political system, and the beginning of that long period of bipartisanship in which Democrats and Republicans, even though they rival one another for political power, will fundamentally act to maintain the control of the society by the wealthy and the privileged.

It's also the opening up of the country to economic forces that are now going to leap ahead. We also now see the consolidation of power by the white man over Indian territory. More land was taken from the Indians during the Civil War than in any other comparable time in American history.

But it's also a period in which the seeds are planted for a kind of protest and organization. The nineteenth century is a time when the labor movement of the North arises, when you are going to see violent strikes against the industrial system, and the struggle for the eight-hour day. In other words, class conflict becomes more intense as the upper class consolidates its power, and the workers in the factories and the farmers in the fields decide that they must organize to do something about their own lives.

If we look at the years right after the Civil War, it seems that there was a lot of idealism injected into American politics. There were the post–Civil War amendments to the Constitution. The work of the Freedmen's Bureau and other voluntary and government-sponsored efforts to resettle former slaves. What happened to all that idealism?

The idealism that brought forth the Thirteenth, Four-teenth, and Fifteenth Amendments collapsed under the weight of political and economic interests. The idealism was sustained in part by realism and necessity and political advantage, which the leaders of Northern society had gained from the temporary alliance with black people. But when they recognized that their fortunes would be better off in alliance with the old white South, then that idealism dissipated.

And yet the idealism of the ex-slaves, and the idealism of those people in the North who cared about racial inequality, that idealism did not disappear. But it was submerged by military and economic power, and by the atmosphere created by the new industrial society.

You might say that the idealists were overwhelmed by the march of the nation toward becoming an economic giant. It took a little while before people began to rebel against this enormous economic power that was developing in the North—the railroads and the banks and the oil industry and the mining industry.

After the Civil War, the economy took off. There was a huge market, and new technological developments brought huge economic growth. It took a while before workers in this new industrial economy were able to gather enough strength to rebel against it.

Now, you give a lot of credit to the abolitionists of the earlier part of the century for creating some of the social consciousness that helped usher in that Civil War period. Many of the same personalities are involved in this imme- diate postwar period. Many of the same structures that abolitionists started earlier in the century led to schools and industrial and vocational institutions throughout the South, and so on. How come they could play such a big role earlier in the century but just couldn't make their presence felt in the 1860s and 1870s?

In the 1860s and 1870s, they had, you might say, a false sense of victory. The technical ending of slavery, the apparent granting of racial equality with the Fourteenth Amendment, and the Fifteenth Amendment giving black people the right to vote all created what I think was a false sense of security for reformist and radical groups in the United States.

A common feature of reform movements is that they become intoxicated with victory and then realize that fol- lowing through on that victory is not going to take place so long as power still remains in the hands of people who held that power earlier.

It took a while to realize that the wave of reform—the Thirteenth, Fourteenth, and Fifteenth Amendments—is going to remain superficial, that those amendments were on the books but were not going to be enforced. The government had the power but wouldn't do it.

There is a certain similarity between the situation there and the situation in the Second Reconstruction, the period of the 1960s when the black movement rose in the South and won victories on the national field. They won the Civil Rights Act of 1964; they won Supreme Court decisions; they won the legal end of segregation. But it turned out that these were insufficient. They didn't speak to the ultimate condition of black people. They didn't change their economic situation. Ultimately, in both periods, it was economic power that determined whether the political reform would have real meaning in the lives of these people who were in a subordinate position.

* * *

Let's turn to the rise of populism and agrarian radicalism later in the century. Who were these radicals out on the farm, and what was their complaint?

We very rarely think of farmers as radicals, but farmers can be radicalized by their condition, by the situation they find themselves in. As the country grew, and as the railroads became more and more monopolized in the hands of a small number of people, individual farmers found themselves powerless before the very wealthy, who controlled what happened to the grain once it came out of the fields and went into the granaries, into the warehouses, and was shipped by railroad to consumers. They found that they were paying high prices for the new farm machinery that was now being used. They had no control over these prices. The federal government was not exercising any control over the power of manufacturers to demand high prices. The farmers had to pay high prices for things that were in the hands of monopolies, and these monopolies could charge high prices without fear of competition. Growers didn't have the power to demand higher prices for their farm products, so they found themselves in very, very difficult economic circumstances in this squeeze.

They realized that as individuals they had no power against powerful economic forces, the railroads and banks that controlled their loans. The only way they could change their situation was to combine, to organize, to do as farmers what workers starting in the 1860s and 1870s had already begun to do—to form labor unions and go on strike.

So the farmers in the 1870s and 1880s began to

organize. They formed granges and farmers alliances. They became a political power in various states, and soon the farmers alliances in the North and South decided that they would form a national political party. They formed what was called the People's Party, which is now known as the Populist Movement.

The People's Party began running candidates for office on the state level, and they elected many candidates to state legislatures in the early 1890s. The Populist Movement became one of the great social movements of American history.

The populists didn't just hold national conventions and put up candidates. They became a cultural force. They distributed thousands of newspapers and gave lectures all over the South. They brought farmers together in a way that they had never been brought together before. And they did something else. For a while, they were able to bring black and white farmers together, unified, to try to get legislation to protect them against the great combines, trusts, and monopolies of that time.

You're talking about a largely unregulated set of industries but also a time when money was tied to the value of gold and silver. It seemed that a set of rules made up for manufacturers and bankers wasn't working so well for people who lived on credit, as farmers did. How did issue of gold and hard money versus paper money, one of the great controversies of the late nineteenth century, land on the shoulders of the individual farmer? What difference did it make to somebody farming wheat in the Great Plains whether or not the American currency was tied to gold and silver?

When money is scarce because it's tied to the gold standard, then people who are debtors, people who owe money, have less and less chance to pay back and to take care of the debts that they have. The constriction of the money supply hurts them.

Farmers want inflation. Inflation is a bad word to consumers, but to people who are in debt, inflation means that money is more available for them to pay off their debts.

This goes back to the period right after the American Revolution, when farmers in the colonies were demanding the issuance of paper money not tied to the gold standard. The counterpart of paper money in the nineteenth century was silver—more plentiful than gold. If silver were used as a standard, the farmers thought, they'd be able to pay off their debts. That's why the Populist Party became the party of silver versus the party of gold.

That's why they ran candidates on a platform of "free silver." Although the farmers themselves did not understand the niceties of finance, they gathered around what seemed like a good slogan: Free Silver. It became the campaign of the Populist Movement when in 1896 it supported Democratic presidential candidate William Jennings Bryan, who ran on the program of free silver.

It's funny, because you could go to national political conventions now and listen to every speech, all day, and not hear anybody mention money, the cost of money, or the basis for money, and yet to be a farmer in the 1880s or 1890s was to be very closely attuned to the status of money.

It is generally not to the advantage of political leaders to have people think too hard about money.

Even today, the working people who are hurt by the tax system, for instance, don't understand the complexities of the tax system. This is to the advantage of those people who promulgate the tax system. The mysteries around money have always served to, I think, diminish the power of working people. It was an unusual moment in the nineteenth century when farmers became conscious of the money situation.

This was also an unusual moment because, for a couple of decades, there was a successful class-based movement that occasionally sought to be also a biracial movement. Why did it eventually fail?

The Populist Movement and the People's Party failed because it poured its energy into politics, into national political campaigns. It allowed itself to be absorbed by the Democratic Party by supporting the candidacy of William Jennings Bryan in 1896. When Bryan lost, the People's Party collapsed. I think the funneling of a movement's energy into the political forum, into the electoral system, diverts that energy from direct action, from struggles in the field. It diverts workers from strikes. I'm just theorizing, because when things like this happen in history, cause and effect are very complex.

Indeed you refer to it as "drowning in a sea of democratic politics," but wasn't that a legitimate strategy? Wouldn't you need members of Congress, governors, members of the Senate, in order to bring the kind of systemic change that would have relieved the burden on the farmers that the coinage problem created?

It is very helpful for movements to have people in political office who will bring about new legislation helpful to the poor, helpful to the farmer, helpful to the worker. However, when that is done at the expense of other forms of struggle, when that depletes the energy of a movement by concentrating it in a sphere where it can immediately be dissipated by a loss, like a loss in an election, then it leaves a movement helpless.

I think that suggests that a very complex and sophisticated strategy is required for social movements, one in which politics and electoral campaigns become part of the struggle but don't dominate it. Because when people engaged in social movements become dependent on political campaigns, they sacrifice something very important. They delude themselves into thinking that passing legislation will change their condition. It will take more than that.

At the same time as the People's Party and agrarian orga-
nizations were rising, so too was the industrial labor
movement, with workers rising up against the conditions
of their employment. But this time, in the late nineteenth
century, those organizations and those uprisings are bet-
ter organized, more sustained, and yes, more violent. Why
then? Why did it happen at that point in American history?

The rise of the labor movement after the Civil War was
directly due to the new conditions in the industrial system,
and to the terrible conditions that existed in the mines.
Industrialization brought about factory work, which was
unregulated. It brought the mining industry into promi-
nence, with no safety precautions in the mines. You have
this enormous economic growth, and in the course of it
the conditions of workers become intensely difficult. This
starts even with the building of the transcontinental railroad in the 1860s, with immigrant workers, Chinese and
Irish workers working very long hours under very difficult conditions, and dying by the thousands as a result of
these conditions.

The industrial system was becoming, you might say,
more cruel. Working conditions were inhumane in

the mines, steel mills, oil refineries, factories, and the meat-packing industry. The demands of the new economy fostered a desire for more and more profit, and in order to profit, you have to get workers who work harder and longer, whose wages are kept as low as possible. Safety costs money. So you get terrible conditions in the mines, in Carnegie's steel mills, in Rockefeller's oil refineries, and in factories throughout the country.

But workers in the mines, factories, and railroads began to talk to one another, and they began to organize unions. After the Civil War, you began to see national unions. The Knights of Labor became a national union, and it's indicative of the problems they faced that the Knights was a secret organization, because the employers don't want workers to organize. Any sign of organization was going to be met with the firing of workers, so people had to organize secretly—until they became strong enough so they could organize overtly and threaten the employer with a strike if anybody was fired for joining the union.

The strike of 1877 was one of the most violent labor strikes in American history, affecting railroads all over the East Coast. A hundred people were killed in clashes between strikers and the military and police.

Then in the 1880s and 1890s, you began to get more strikes. In the early 1890s, the American Federation of Labor was formed, and you began to get more and more worker organizations. There were more strikes, notably of dock workers in New Orleans and steelworkers in Pennsylvania, and then came the great Pullman strike.

The Pullman Palace Car Company prided itself on these beautiful train cars that the wealthy could ride in, but the people who made those cars were not getting enough money to live on. When they went out on strike, something unusual happened. They called upon railroad workers all over the country to join them, not just other Pullman workers. The American Railway Union, headed by Eugene Debs, decided to organize a national boycott of the railroads, and so you had a national railroad strike in 1894.

The strike was eventually broken, as most strikes are broken, by a combination of military force and judicial edict. The courts said, "You must not make any more speeches calling on people to strike or supporting the strike," and when Eugene Debs continued to support the strikers, well, they said he was violating an injunction, and so he went to prison.

* * *

One of the best-known organizers of that time was Mother Jones. Who was she? How did she get her start at a time when women were not known to be political actors on the national stage?

Mary Jones was her name. She grew up in the Midwest and worked as a domestic in menial jobs, developing a class consciousness that soon brought her into the mine workers union.

In her seventies (and I guess this was one of the reasons she was called Mother, because she was old enough to be the mother of almost everybody who was working), she was organizing miners in West Virginia, and then Colorado. She was so colorful and so dramatic, and she looked like a schoolteacher, wearing her bonnet over her white hair.

She was a fiery speaker. She did very dramatic things, like bringing the children of striking miners in Pennsylvania on a march to New York, to Theodore Roosevelt's house, to demand an end to child labor. They were carrying signs saying WE WANT TIME TO PLAY.

Mother Jones came to Colorado in 1913, when the

coal miners of Colorado went out on strike against the Rockefeller-owned mines of southern Colorado. Her coming galvanized the miners. She showed up at the Miners Convention in Trinidad, Colorado, when they were deciding whether to strike, and she gave a rousing speech. They went out on strike.

She was jailed many times. Nothing daunted her. She was brought into courts and she would defy the judge. She inspired miners and other workers all over the country.

Once organized workers realized that companies and governments were willing to use force, willing to kill them to stop strikes, to end disruptions in service on the railroads, was there a change in tactics?

Workers saw from the beginning that force would be employed against them. I don't know if there was a change in tactics throughout the labor movement, but I would say that certain parts of the labor movement decided that they had to meet force with force. There were the Molly Maguires of Pennsylvania. There were workers who turned to force under certain conditions.

The National Guard, paid by Rockefeller, attacked the large tent colony in which striking miners were living, at

Ludlow, Colorado. They burned the tents to the ground and machine-gunned the tents, and in one of the tents they found the burned bodies of eleven children and two women. Those victims suddenly brought the strike into national attention, and that incident became known as the Ludlow Massacre. Woody Guthrie wrote a song about it called "The Ludlow Massacre."

That action galvanized the miners into violence. They had not been violent up to that point, but now this was too much, the attack on the Ludlow tent colony. An enormous funeral parade took place in Trinidad, a town that's the center of the mining district, with the coffins of these eleven children and two women, as well as seven other people who had died at the hands of the National Guard. There was this odd juxtaposition—the solemn procession behind these coffins and then the workers leaving the procession and going into certain houses and taking rifles that had been stored there, and then going on a violent rampage through the mining district, blowing up mines and killing mine guards.

This was a spontaneous violent reaction, and I suppose what I am saying is that, while the labor movement as a whole has not engaged in violence as a general tactic, there have been individual times, instances, when certain parts of the labor movement had been willing to use violence. The IWW [Industrial Workers of the World], a radical labor union in the early twentieth century, was not as restrained as the American Federation of Labor. They believed in fighting back. They believed in sabotage, destroying property if necessary, as a tactic to combat the power of the employer. But I think it is fair to say that, in general, the labor movement was nonviolent.

*   *   *

The roughly twenty-five years from the Haymarket battle in Chicago to the election of Woodrow Wilson is often called the Progressive Period or the Progressive Era. Does it deserve the name, and are there things from that time that endure?

From the Haymarket Affair in 1886 to the election of Woodrow Wilson in 1912—to call those years the Progressive Period is a terrible commentary on the way we see history.

For one thing, that was the period of the greatest number of lynchings of black people in American history. An African American historian named Rayford Logan wrote a book about that period. He called it *The Nadir*, the low point in the history of race in the United States. So that is one way of looking at the Progressive Period.

Another thing that casts doubt on the name "Progressive Period" is that this was also a period of very intense labor struggles and very intense exploitation of labor. Immigrants were coming into the country and going to work in the mines and mills and factories. They were crowding into cities festering with disease and bad water. Lots of children were dying in the winter of cold and pneumonia. Hardly a progressive period.

It was called the Progressive Period for the same reason we very often give unlikely names to other historical periods. Because in the early twentieth century, some reform laws were passed by Congress—including the Federal Reserve Act, the Sixteenth and Seventeenth Amendments to the Constitution, the graduated income tax, and direct election of the Senate. You could point to certain progressive pieces of legislation, but the conditions of workers in factories, the conditions of people living in the slums of the cities—these did not warrant calling this the Progressive Period.

Now, sure, some things happened during that period

that would give you some sense of the possibilities of change, some sense that people could react to their situation. I'm thinking now of the labor movement. I'm thinking of the rise of the Socialist Party. I'm thinking of the rise of the IWW. And of course it was at this time, in 1909, that the NAACP was formed.

The Socialist Party, the IWW, and the NAACP are indicators that, in one of the worst periods of American history, black people and working people did not simply take their situation passively. They rebelled.

The same period was also one of the great high tides of American immigration. August Spies, one of those charged in the Haymarket bombings, Emma Goldman, Samuel Gompers, John Lewis, Joe Hill, and a little later Marcus Garvey—they're all immigrants. Many of them are American radicals, labor organizers. They're movement leaders. But they also came to these shores from other places in the world. Not just a coincidence, is it?

No, it's not a coincidence, because people who were forced out of other places in the world, or left voluntarily because they didn't like what they were living through in those places, came to this country hoping that they would find a society that welcomed them. Instead, they found conditions as horrendous as conditions back in Europe.

Now, there were some immigrants who simply went back. One of the untold stories of American immigration is the percentage of immigrants who went back to their own countries after experiencing what was supposed to be the glories of American society.

But some of those who stayed became rebels against this society. You mention the name of August Spies, an anarchist, a radical, from Germany. Like other immigrants, he came to the United States hoping to find a better society, a more welcoming society, but instead he found exploitation of labor here, and the rule of the rich. He joined with other anarchists in Chicago in the 1880s, and they were quite a militant group.

Spies was one of the eight anarchist leaders who were rounded up in 1886 at the time of the Haymarket Affair. The Haymarket Affair is the name given to an event that occurred in early May 1886, when working people gathered in Haymarket Square in Chicago to protest the police killing of strikers that had taken place a few days before, during a demonstration for the eight-hour day.

This gathering of people at the Haymarket, which was

addressed by anarchist leaders and other people, was attacked by the police although they were doing nothing but speaking. They were doing nothing violent. A great squadron of police marched onto the scene and attacked them. As the police advanced on the protesters, a bomb was thrown into the midst of the police, killing seven of them.

The reaction of Chicago's political leadership and police was to immediately go out and arrest eight anarchists, none of whom could be found to have anything to do with the bomb. The idea was that whoever threw the bomb was probably incited by these anarchists, who called in no uncertain terms for meeting violence with violence.

Most of the eight anarchist leaders were foreign-born, with the exception of Albert Parsons, who was an important leader of the anarchist and labor movement in Chicago, and who actually had fought in the Civil War on the side of the Confederacy. He was a Southerner, but somehow he became radicalized as a labor leader and anarchist.

These eight men were sentenced to death, and in fact four of them were executed, including Parsons and August

Spies. The execution of these four resounded very power-fully among class-conscious working people throughout the country.

You can find a kind of current that runs from one event to another, and from one event to another person's con-sciousness. I'm thinking of Emma Goldman, who was to become an outrageous figure in early twentieth-century history, an anarchist feminist. Emma Goldman was a teenager working in a factory in Rochester, New York, when she learned of the execution of the four anarchists in Haymarket. She was not an anarchist. She was just a worker who was very intelligent and very keenly con-scious of the terrible conditions under which working people lived.

The Haymarket Affair sparked something in her. It pro-voked her to leave her family and leave her job in Roch-ester to go to New York and meet with a little group of anarchists, and then to become a speaker, an organizer, a remarkable figure. She spoke out for garment workers in New York, against the terrible factory conditions, and for birth control and the rights of women. She was jailed many, many times. She remains today one of the relatively unknown figures in American history and yet to me is a very heroic figure. I went all through graduate school studying American history, and the name of Emma Goldman was never mentioned. As happens so often, you have to leave the classroom and go to the library.

So from that radicalizing experience of hearing about the Haymarket martyrs, Emma Goldman embarked on a long public career.

Yes, if the word *career* applies to a radical agitator and organizer. Emma Goldman went on from being angered by the execution of the anarchists in Chicago to become a very important figure in the history of American radicalism.

She gave a fiery speech during the economic crisis of 1893 in Union Square, speaking to a huge number of people. People were starving at that time, and one third of the working population was unemployed. In effect, she said, "Don't bother petitioning, don't bother trying to get laws passed. We need something right away. If your kids need food, go into the stores and take it."

That is what anarchists believed in. They believed in direct action. They didn't believe in petitions and lobbying, or voting and waiting for the right person to be voted into office to do the right thing. They believed in immediately acting against the source of the problem.

Emma Goldman went to prison many times. For that speech in Union Square, she was sentenced to two years in Blackwell's Island. In 1892, she'd become involved in a plot to assassinate Henry Clay Frick.

Frick was manager of Carnegie Steel Company plants in Pittsburgh. There was a strike in Pittsburgh, and striking workers were gunned down. A little group of anarchists, including Emma Goldman, decided that, to show that the working class did not have to take their own victimization calmly, as a symbolic act, they would assassinate Henry Clay Frick.

Alexander Berkman was Emma Goldman's companion and lover for a while, and one of those New York anarchists. He went to Pittsburgh to kill Frick. He was a good anarchist but a very poor shot. He failed and was sent to prison for a long time.

But Emma Goldman went on. She was so notorious that when President McKinley was assassinated in 1901, they immediately started looking for Emma Goldman, thinking that whoever assassinated McKinley, he had been provoked by somebody like her.

She played an important role in those early years of the twentieth century, but finally in World War I she reached the end of her activity when she was imprisoned for speaking out against the war. She and Alexander Berkman were both sent to prison, and when they got out, they were deported from the United States back to where they had been born, in Russia. FBI director J. Edgar Hoover himself went to the dock to make sure that they were put on the boat and sent out of the country.

Are these movements—the socialist movement, anarchism—are they American things, or are they kind of world hybrids? Rebels, radicals of various stripes had been pouring into the United States—the Sons of Ireland [Young Ireland], after their failed uprising on the island of Ireland, the refugees from the revolutions of 1848, Paris Communards, Giuseppe Garibaldi, José Martí, Leon Trotsky even—all were coming to the New World. Did they leave an influence that makes this not, strictly speaking, a totally American thing?

Well, certainly not a totally American thing. But also not a totally foreign thing.

It's easy to put down these radical movements by saying

these are just foreign agitators. The idea of maintaining control by ascribing opposition to foreign influence goes back to the period right after the American Revolution, when the Alien and Sedition Acts were passed and when revolutionary attitudes were ascribed to Irishmen who had just come back from Ireland, where they had been agitating for Irish independence from England, and to Frenchmen who were refugees from the French Revolution. So this was an old story.

It's true that August Spies and Samuel Fielden and other members of the Haymarket group were from Europe. On the other hand, there was Parsons, who was a native-born American. There were foreign-born anarchists and also native-born anarchists. It has always been a mixture of native-born and foreign-born bound together in a common cause.

In the early days of the American labor movement, one of the tried and true ways to break strikes, to bust up organizing efforts, was to use either black people or immigrant scabs as strikebreakers. Why was that such an effective tactic?

It was effective for a couple of reasons. One, these

immigrants were desperate for work, and black people were in the lowest economic strata. So if you offered them a wage higher than they'd been getting, they'd go to work and take the place of strikers.

Often they weren't even told what they were doing. In the Colorado coal strike of 1914, strikebreakers—black and white—were brought in on trains whose windows were blacked out so they couldn't see picketing going on. They were very often deceived. But it was most often desperation that led them to take the place of strikers.

Of course, this was also a way of building up anger and animosity between two groups of people both of whom really were the victims of the capitalist system. For the corporations and the employer class, it was useful and practical to hire immigrants and Negroes as strikebreakers.

It didn't always work. There were times when black people and white people got together, as they did in New Orleans at the turn of the century. In the textile strike of 1912, the workers themselves were immigrants.

In one of its most glorious moments, the IWW played a role in bringing varied immigrant groups together in Lawrence, Massachusetts, in 1912, and holding out against the American Woolen Company and the other textile manufacturers, leading the strikers to victory. A victorious strike was a rare thing.

A century after the high-water mark of American social-ism, why is it almost a secret that there were Socialist members of Congress and state legislatures and Debs got millions of votes for president?

The word *socialism* has lost its glamour. In the early part of the twentieth century, when the Socialist Party was a force and when people were elected as Socialists, socialism was something romantic and idealistic. It rep-resents the idea of equality, the idea of companionship, of people getting together.

The Soviet Union's emergence onto the world scene in the Bolshevik Revolution in 1917, I believe, was the most important factor in leading to a new, very negative view of the very idea of socialism. It's also true that the Social-ist Party was broken by the attacks on it in World War I, when so many of its leaders went to prison for oppos-ing the war. They came out of that period very much beaten back.

But the Soviet Union became the representative of socialism—and a more and more obviously poor one.

In the 1930s and 1940s, when Stalinism became more clearly understood as a dictatorship—not a benign dictatorship of the proletariat as perhaps Marx had envisioned, but a dictatorship *over* the proletariat—it was very hard to expect people to gather around socialism as a unifying word.

However, to jump decades ahead, to 1989 and 1990 and the breakup of the Soviet Union, I think the fall of the Soviet Union created a new opening for the idea of socialism, because socialism had become identified with Stalinism, with tyranny and the gulag. The disappearance of the Soviet Union created an opportunity for socialism to reconstitute itself as an idea—to look back to the time of Eugene Debs, Mother Jones, Emma Goldman, Clarence Darrow, Jack London, Helen Keller, and the many other very famous Americans who were socialists.

* * *

During this same period that we've been talking about, the United States embarked on military actions overseas. It began with the war against Spain in 1898 and continued with the suppression of the Philippine rebellion and their war for independence. It then continued in Haiti,

Nicaragua, throughout the Caribbean. What was going on there?

What is called the Age of Imperialism is seen as starting in 1898 with the Spanish-American War, that is, a war in Cuba against Spain.

But I think it's fair to say that American imperialism started long before that. It started with the march across the continent, with the seizing of Indian lands. It started with one of the major ethnic cleansings, to use a current expression, of modern history—the taking away from the Indians of this enormous expanse of territory and turning that land over to white Americans who were moving westward from the Atlantic Ocean. The war with Mexico was part of that expansion. Manifest Destiny, the idea that it was the work of Providence, of God ordaining the United States government to become a mighty continental power from the Atlantic to the Pacific and down to the Gulf of Mexico—all that predated the Spanish-American War.

With the country now so large, and with industries turning out goods for which the domestic market was insufficient, and where there was a greater demand for the raw materials possessed by other countries, U.S. political and military leaders began to look overseas.

Cuba was a natural first target. It was so close, and there was a good excuse—that Spain was occupying Cuba. This has been a constant in American expansionism, finding a kind of humanitarian excuse. Of course, there is a half truth to it in that the Spanish were cruel occupiers of Cuba. And the United States did in fact, in a short war—what Secretary of State John Hay called a "splendid little war"—drive Spain out of Cuba.

Spain was gone. The United States and American corporations were in. United Fruit was in. American banks were in. American railroads were in. And the United States wrote parts of the Cuban constitution, giving it the right to intervene militarily in Cuba anytime.

This was the beginning of overseas expansion by the United States. At the very end of the war in Cuba, the United States turned its attention to the Philippines. While the 1898 war in Cuba is given a lot of attention in American history books, with a kind of romantic attention to Theodore Roosevelt marching up San Juan Hill and the Rough Riders and all that, the Philippine War is barely mentioned. Yet the Spanish-American War lasted three months, and the Philippine War lasted for years and years. And it was a bloody war in which at least half a million Filipinos died.

The war in the Philippines was in many ways a preview of the Vietnam War. Here was the United States sending an army and navy halfway around the world to subdue a local population. President McKinley explained his decision to take over the Philippines by saying that he got down on his knees and prayed to God to tell him what to do about the Philippines and God told him that it was his duty to civilize and Christianize the Filipinos. The Filipinos, of course, got a different message from God. They rebelled, holding out for years until they were finally subdued. There followed fifty years of American military occupation, and dictatorship after dictatorship in the Philippines.

This was only the start. In 1915, Woodrow Wilson sent an army into Haiti, the first black republic in the Western Hemisphere. Several thousand Haitians were killed, and the American occupation of Haiti lasted for nearly two decades. Wilson also sent troops into the Dominican Republic, another long occupation. This pattern of American military intervention in other countries continued. All through the early twentieth century, the marines were sent into countries in Central America, to Nicaragua and Panama.

But isn't there something very different about the way the United States goes about this projection of power—unlike the British, who brought a state church and their flag and their laws and their army to India, Nigeria, southern Africa, East Africa; unlike the French, who colonized North Africa and parts of the Caribbean, and had members of their Chamber of Deputies who had seats in these far-flung places throughout the world. The United States didn't annex or colonize Liberia or the Philippines or Central America or Venezuela or any of the other places in which Americans had extensive commercial interests. They just did business.

The United States came late onto the imperial scene. By the time the United States moved out of its continental limits into the world, it already had behind it the experiences of the older empires, of the British and French and German empires.

U.S. leaders understood that they didn't have to colonize these places in the same way, so long as they controlled their economies and so long as the American military was ready to move in at crucial times to make sure governments were in power that would be friendly to American business interests.

For instance, in Central America and in the Caribbean, you don't find colonization in the same way that the British colonized India or East Africa. But you find the marines moving into every country in Central America whenever there is a threat to a government that the United States is confident about, friendly with, and accustomed to.

And you do find periods of occupation. You find the United States going into Haiti in 1915 and staying there until 1934. When the Haitians rebel against American occupation, they are put down. This happens under Woodrow Wilson—and here's another example of history being distorted. Wilson is portrayed generally in history as an idealist and a sort of moral person who is associated with the League of Nations and so on, but Wilson was ruthless in occupying Haiti and the Dominican Republic and in sending warships to Mexico to bombard the Mexican coast.

It was a more sophisticated kind of imperialism, but imperialism nevertheless. And today American imperialism takes the form of military bases all over the world, of American corporations being dominant in the affairs of other countries. It is in many ways a more pervasive kind of imperialism than existed in the old order and maybe more effective, because it doesn't involve a constant occupation of troops, like the British occupying India. It only requires the occasional occupation of countries when other methods fail.

Nevertheless, American imperialism has the same fundamental characteristic of traditional European imperialism: the control of other people's economies for the benefit of American business interests.

Now, in many of these cases—certainly in the Spanish-American War of 1898, again in putting down the rebellion in the Philippines, again in the American incursion into northern Mexico during the Civil War there—black troops were used very heavily by the American military. Did that have repercussions at home?

The use of black troops in the Philippines *did* have repercussions in the United States, as well as causing dissension in the ranks of soldiers in the Philippines. That was the result of black soldiers hearing their white fellow soldiers call the Filipinos niggers—and this very blatant racism in the American army shocked the black soldiers.

These black soldiers wrote letters to African American newspapers back in the United States complaining about this. And they were learning from the people back home about the riots and lynchings going on. Here were black soldiers supposedly fighting for freedom and democracy, and meanwhile members of their families were being lynched.

So there *were* repercussions. Part of the reason for the Niagara Movement and rising of the NAACP was this consciousness of imperialism, this consciousness of American power being used against people of color in other places in the world.

* * *

Should stories of resistance like the ones you've been telling force us to rethink conventional American history?

If you leave out the history of resistance, then what you get out of American history is a kind of toothless history. You get a history in which everything seems okay. You get the kind of history that leads Americans to say to one another, "This is the greatest country in the world. We have always done good things in the world." Then they're surprised when the United States is criticized by people in other countries.

Many Americans grow up believing that we have done nothing but good in the world. Then if they learn that we have in fact been an imperialist nation, that corporations have exploited the working class, and that we have a long history of slavery and racism, well, that is an awakening of consciousness. It's very important, then, for people who are conscious of victimization to also become conscious of the fact that the victims did not always accept their situation humbly. That they resisted. That we had strikes and riots, and desertions from the army, and movements against the war. It's important for Americans to know this, so that they understand that it is possible for people to resist. Whether Americans remain passive in the face of a government that ruins America's reputation by what it does abroad, whether Americans remain passive in the face of a small number of powerful and rich people who seize control of the government and use it for their purposes—whether Americans remain passive in the face of all this is in part determined by what they know of their history.

People are desperately in need of support if they want

to resist powers that are essentially immoral. They can get some of that support by learning this history of resistance, all through the American past.

I'm going to guess it's quite difficult for a lot of Americans to square what they know of their own family history with this story of oppressors and victims and resisters. People don't think of their Scandinavian forebears who were given farms by the American government in the Great Plains as oppressors; they think of them as people who went and farmed. People don't think of their Slavic coal-miner ancestors or their Hungarian steelworker ancestors in Cleveland, or even more recent arrivals, as shareholders in a story of exploitation and oppression.

It's certainly true that, for many people in this country, the history of their families is a story of success. Many people now own their own homes, can afford to go on vacation, and have cars and television sets and cell phones, all the paraphernalia of modern civilization. That is the great American middle class.

But there is also a very large underclass of people who are living under terrible conditions. They live in bad housing in cities all over the country, with inadequate medical care or none. These people work long hours for very little and have trouble feeding their families.

We have a middle class. I think that explains the lack of a revolutionary movement in the United States. That explains the relative stability of the American system. There obviously have been signs of rebellion and struggle, but still the system has maintained stability, and one of the reasons is that it has offered something to enough Americans to make them supporters of the system. And you might say they act as a buffer between the small number of very rich people and the large number who are desperate and struggling. So yes, I think we have to see both sides of this. We cannot explain the continued power of wealth in the American political system without understanding that the wealthy have been able to use the middle class, which has done pretty well, as a support for itself. The American system is ingenious, as it constantly skims off part of the working class and brings them into the middle class, making rebellion harder.

I see this, for instance, in what has happened to the black movement in this country. At the end of the period of the civil rights movement, the United States had a substantial black middle class—not a large part of the black population, perhaps 10 or 15 percent, but enough to take the edge off black rebellion. So black people moved into the business world, more of them went to college, more of them appeared on television and in media.

And yet 75 or 80 percent of the population still live in difficult circumstances. All you have to do is walk through any American city, and you'll see a microcosm of American life. When you walk through the city of Boston, where I live, you'll walk through neighborhoods that match your description of the contented American, the successful American—neighborhoods where people live in nice houses.

Then, if you're a good walker, if you're persistent, you will soon come to parts of the city that look as if a war has taken place there. You'll see broken-down homes, you'll see littered streets, and you'll see the signs of unemployment. I am sure this is true not just in Boston; it's true in New York, in Chicago, in Detroit and Los Angeles.

This country has the wealth to take care of everybody, to give everybody free health care, to give everybody free university education, to give everybody good housing. But it doesn't do that, and this is probably in part because of the existence of this contented middle class.

You've just given us a tour of the vast divergence of interests, the different groups in the population opposed to each other, having mutually exclusive visions of the future. So, in your view, is there such a thing as an American national interest?

I don't think there is a national interest. I think national interest is an example of one of those terms that's used to suggest a unity of interests that doesn't exist.

This starts right from the beginning, with the Founding Fathers. It starts with the Constitution, with the first words in the preamble to the Constitution, "We the People establish this constitution," because it wasn't "We the People," it was fifty-five rich white men gathered in Philadelphia. There was no unified interest at that time. There were the slave owners and the slaves. There were the landlords and the tenants. There were the rich and the poor.

Those words "We the People" were a way of deceiving people into thinking that there was a national interest. The term *national interest* is what the novelist Kurt Vonnegut called a granfalloon (this is one of his invented words), which is sort of an artificial constellation of people, people who are artificially brought together but really don't have any common interests.

I think that in order for Americans to progress, to change things, to not become victims anymore, they have to recognize that there are different interests—differences in status, differences in income—which if not recognized simply contribute to freezing the status quo.

We talked about the way Manifest Destiny jumped the border and headed out into the developing world in the early years of the twentieth century. Is the U.S. entry into World War I part of that same story?

The entry into World War I is another example of the pretense that we're going to war for one reason, while there are other reasons that are not given to the American public. The pretense was that we were going to war because we wanted to make the world safe for democracy and because the Germans were attacking our ships on the high seas.

It's interesting how often, in preparing the nation to go to war, a president first declares his intention not to go to war at all—because there is, I believe, a natural disinclination on the part of the public to send their young people to war. In 1916, Wilson was reelected president with the slogan "There is such a thing as being too proud to fight."

Wilson was not going to get us into war in 1916, but then he's elected, and in 1917 he gets us into war. It was presented as total evil on one side and total good on the other side. The Kaiser was total evil, and had committed atrocities. Our side, the British and French side, was okay. Of course, on our side was the British Empire and the French Empire, people who massacred the native people in India and Africa. Part of the propaganda was that the Germans were committing atrocities against the Belgians, but Belgium was responsible for the deaths of at least a million people in the Belgian Congo.

My point is that this was a war of imperial countries against one another, fighting for possession and control of various parts of the world. But it was presented as a war for democracy and liberty.

In World War I, over four years of war, 10 million soldiers died. And at the end of it, nobody could really figure out why the war was fought.

There was a movement inside the United States of resistance against the war. The Socialist Party and the IWW both opposed it. Two thousand people were prosecuted for speaking out against the war. Congress had passed the Espionage Act, which was not really about espionage.

The Espionage Act made it a crime to say anything or print anything that would discourage recruitment or enlistment in the armed forces. If you spoke out against the war, against American entrance into World War I, you were violating the Espionage Act. Eugene Debs made a speech in Ohio against the war, and he was sentenced to ten years in prison.

PART III

"They Began to Organize":
The Twentieth Century and Beyond

What happened in the 1921 Tulsa Race Riot? And maybe you could also tell me what life was like for black people in places like Oklahoma at that time.

The Tulsa Race Riot is one of those events like so many—very dramatic, very important, and yet somehow not mentioned in traditional histories. The memory of it was actually wiped out. It was part of a wave of anti-black riots that took place in the United States right after World War I. There had been another really deadly attack against black people in East St. Louis in 1917, but after the war there were many such riots all over the country.

They usually started with one incident that fueled anger and hysteria. In this case, a black kid in Tulsa was accused of molesting a white woman. It was very unclear whether this had really happened or not, but a number of black people gathered around where this kid was being held to protect him from lynching. They were armed, because they expected trouble. Seventy-five black people were there, but about fifteen hundred armed whites gathered around and immediately rampaged. And essentially the black neighborhood in Tulsa was destroyed. It was really as if a war had taken place. How many people died in that riot, nobody knows exactly.

Then the records were destroyed. It seemed like a scene out of Gabriel García Márquez, where a huge massacre takes place, and then all evidence of it is gone. And nobody seems to want to know about it.

These riots had a very powerful effect on the black community. I suspect that some of the important literature and art that came out of the black community after the war was in some way inspired and provoked by what happened. After the riot in East St. Louis in 1917, the great black performer Josephine Baker went to France. She said, "The very idea of America makes me shake and tremble and gives me nightmares."

One thing they have in common—they seem to come at a time when these black communities that are attached to part of the commercial life of midsize cities around the country, when the population gets to a certain level, there is a growing sense of the presence of this parallel black city within a city. Then with the excuse of sexual indiscretion running like a strong undercurrent, involving young black men and white women, it starts. Even though its roots seem to have more to do with real estate and population levels than with sex, sex is often the excuse. It's almost pathological.

There is nothing that arouses hatred more than the idea that some alien person, some person of another race, has somehow violated people in your pure race. So yes, sex has been very often a critical element in the beginning of a riot or some sort of outbreak of violence. But economics is very important in all of this. Sex may have been the excuse, but very often there were other resentments. Very often it was the fact that whites were having trouble getting jobs and they saw black people coming in and taking their jobs.

As we look back over the history of the last century, should we be focused more on the fact that this history was almost completely erased and lost, or more on the fact that now people are in good faith trying to re-create the story—to find out exactly what happened and why it happened?

I think both are important. I think it is important to know and to be conscious of how important events in history are erased. We should be conscious of the stories today that may be wiped out of memory ten years from now, because the problem of obliterating pieces of the past is not a problem of the past. It is a continuing problem.

It's important to be aware of the fact that you have been deprived of important pieces of history. At a certain point you begin to learn about these things. It gives you at least a modicum of confidence that, after a while, the erased is beginning to reappear and it's possible to begin to unearth things that were intended to be buried.

White people of goodwill are involved in this project, too, not just black people trying to document their own past.

There is no question that white people of goodwill and black people have both worked to reconstitute those events that have been hidden from view. And that is encouraging. There were always white people in the South who understood what was going on and tried in some way to counteract that.

* * *

*The conventional tellings of American history often por-
tray the Great Depression as an aberration, a sudden
descent into economic calamity from the relatively prosperous efflorescence of the Jazz Age. But in* A People's
History, *you tell a very different story about the roots of
the Great Depression being very much in the 1920s.*

The idea that the Great Depression of the 1930s was an
aberration in an otherwise prolonged march of prosperity
in the United States is itself simply false. There had been
depressions, and severe ones, all through American history from the early nineteenth century on. The Depression of 1873 was one of the causes of the Great Railroad
Strike of 1877. There was a Great Depression in 1893; I
mentioned the fact that Emma Goldman was imprisoned
for addressing people in New York who were in desperate
trouble because of the economic crisis of 1893.

I became aware of this myself after studying history—
and you would think that somebody who studies history
on the graduate level is now really a master and knows
everything. Of course, what you discover is that there
are things you don't know, things that even your most

advanced courses in history would not tell you. I did not learn a certain important truth about the pre-Depression years, about the 1920s, until I began doing research on the life and career of Fiorello La Guardia. I was doing my doctoral dissertation and I came across the papers of Fiorello La Guardia, which had just been deposited in the Municipal Archives of New York City by his widow.

La Guardia was a congressman in the 1920s, representing a district in East Harlem. I was reading all of the letters that had been sent to La Guardia in the 1920s, in the age of prosperity, the Jazz Age, this period that still is remembered that way. There were people writing letters saying, "My husband is out of work. They have turned off the electricity, 'cause we can't pay the bill. My kids are going hungry." And when I looked into other parts of the country, I realized that although it wasn't a depression in the strictest sense, the 1920s was a period of great wealth on one side and poverty on another side.

What that did for me—and I think this is what history very often does—was make me wonder if what I had learned about that period was true also of other periods.

I was writing about this in the 1950s, and I realized that the 1950s are not considered a period of tough economic deprivation for most Americans. But I wondered, is there an underside to the 1950s? I read Michael Harrington's book *The Other America*, and that is exactly what he was talking about. Here in the so-called prosperous 1950s there were people suffering all over the country. So yes, the Great Depression was indeed a low point, but it doesn't mean that the other periods preceding it and after it were high points.

It's funny how master narratives get built, and even in the face of all kinds of other evidence, you just can't pierce the armor of that master narrative. When you think about the sepia-toned silent movie footage that runs through Jazz Age storytelling, those people doing the Charleston, the tops being knocked off of champagne bottles, and so on—they don't intersperse that with mounted soldiers ousting people out of tents during the Bonus Marches. Those Bonus Marchers were workingmen who just couldn't make it in 1920s America.

It's interesting that you talk about the Bonus Army, because that is certainly something known to people who know history. But most Americans don't know about the Bonus Army, even though it was a very, very dramatic moment in American history at the very beginning of the Great Depression.

It was only thirteen years after the end of World War I, and these veterans were now probably in their thirties, and they had families. And they were suffering. They had been promised money, they had been promised a bonus, as veterans are always given promises.

If you are going to risk your limbs, you have to be given promises, so the veterans had been given promises that at least they would get a bonus after the war. But a bonus was never given to them, and now that they were hungry, they organized what was called a Bonus Army. They came from all over the country, thousands of them, came in every which way they could—riding the rails, hitchhiking, whatever. They arrived in Washington and encamped across the Potomac River from the Capitol. They set up tents there, and they wanted to be a visible presence in Washington, to say to Congress, "We want our bonus."

Herbert Hoover was president. I don't know if any other president would have behaved differently. I don't know, if we had had a Democratic president at that time, if he would have behaved differently. But what Hoover did was to send the army to destroy their camp and drive them out of there. It was one of the most shameful episodes in modern American history.

Now, maybe it had some effect on Franklin D. Roosevelt. Maybe he decided when he came into office in 1933 that you couldn't simply send the army to suppress people who were in dire economic straits. I think Roosevelt was more sensitive than Hoover, and probably Roosevelt was more sensitive than any president that followed him in regard to the plight of people.

The country was in turmoil in the 1930s when Roosevelt came into office. There were strikes all over the country. There were riots. There were people breaking into places where there was food. There were children marching into city halls demanding that they be fed and taken care of. Tenants were organizing and refusing to be evicted, bringing furniture back into the homes after it had been taken out to the street. It was a country that was in a state of near-revolution, something that very much worried the people in Washington.

Certainly Roosevelt was sensitive to this. The New Deal was the result of it—the result of the combination of Roosevelt's sensitivity and the events, the uproar, the rebellions taking place all over the country, which he had to take notice of.

It sounds as though, in part, you think the New Deal was done to forestall revolution. I guess historians have different points of view that we could graph out on a continuum, from the belief that he saved the country because he wanted to save the people, to a more cynical take that he saved capitalism because he realized it was having a nervous breakdown but really wasn't all that interested in saving the people per se.

I would probably argue that there was truth in both sides. This sounds as if I am a moderate, compromising, finding the center between two points of view, but I wouldn't give equal weight to both analyses. I think, yes, Roosevelt was saving capitalism, no question about that—and I think he was conscious of that too.

I think he was saving the system that he believed in from revolution, from very deep trouble, but I think he also was a human being responding to the plight of people. He may not have responded so easily if there hadn't been all this turmoil and threat to the system, but there was something in Roosevelt that wanted to do some good.

I think probably one of the elements that should be considered in assessing Roosevelt is that he had a wife, Eleanor Roosevelt, who was actually more sensitive than he was to the plight of poor people. She had been a social worker on the Lower East Side of New York; she had actually been among the poor. You can't say this about Roosevelt himself. She had a better grasp of how poor people lived, of how black people were suffering in a racist society, and I think she was a good influence on Franklin Roosevelt.

The personal reminiscences of people who lived through those times feature a very strong narrative undercurrent of "We did what we had to to get through." There was a lot of sharing, a lot of digging deep and figuring out ways to get over—a story of self-reliance, you might say. How does that mesh with the tremendous flowering at the same time of relief programs, of direct supply of nutrition, of work, of public works projects and all that? How do those two narratives move together on parallel tracks?

People like to think of themselves as self-reliant. It's a part of American culture that people will take care of themselves, will not depend on other people, but will take a certain pride in not being dependent on the government.

But it's also true that when people become desperate enough, that pride and self-reliance break down. They will accept the fact that, for survival, they need the government. My family was a poor family, a working-class family, living in Brooklyn at that time. My father and mother were both garment workers, then factory workers. Then my father was a waiter. Now, in the Depression, he couldn't find jobs as a waiter. And they were proud people. They had always worked hard to keep the family alive.

I have a vivid memory of seeing my mother standing on the line where they were giving out food baskets. When later I reminded my mother of that, I recall that she shook her head. She said, "No, I never did that."

But the New Deal also fostered a kind of cooperation and collectivity. When I spoke about the people in the neighborhood getting together to stop an eviction, to bring furniture of an evicted family back into the house— this was people helping one another.

New Deal programs brought people together. The WPA brought people together on work projects, whether it was planting trees or cleaning up places in the country. The

Federal Arts Program was a magnificent achievement of the New Deal, which has not been matched since, because for the first time artists were not simply left to the whims of the free market.

The New Deal brought writers together in cooperative enterprises, producing books. It brought artists together, making murals. It brought people together in the theater, creating hundreds of plays under the Federal Theatre Project.

So it was a period where you might say, in a certain sense, people learned to rely on government help, but they also developed in many ways a very warm, cooperative spirit.

I find the stories that people tell of that time to be as revealing as what really happened. I wonder sometimes if that story of self-reliance in the Depression gives us a problem in seeing what really happened. Rarely do you hear people talk about the unusual level of family dissolution that went on during those times. Men in the hundreds of thousands walked out of homes, left children, left wives. There were small armies of unattached children in the big cities of America, young people who had nobody looking out for them, in part because of the economic calamity of that time.

We really were having a social nervous breakdown. Seattle, San Francisco, New York, and other big port cities were filling up with unattached men. Railroad camps were filled with family men who now were suddenly at loose ends.

By telling ourselves that we hunkered down and pulled through, don't we sort of blunt the heartbreaking, horrifying truth of what went on during the economic meltdown?

It is very hard to recapture the real depth of suffering and the breakup of family ties that happened. People left their homes and went to other places in the country to find work. Families were broken up, and children were given over to other families or were left to the care of the state. So, yes, the real intensity of those stories sometimes gets lost as time goes on, and the retelling loses some of the reality.

* * *

Moving ahead to World War II, which is often called the Good War. It is often remembered as one of the times

*when people stood shoulder to shoulder and the country
was unified against a common enemy.*

*But one part of the story that sort of sticks out is the
internment of Japanese Americans and Japanese nation-
als living in the United States. Is that all of a piece, in
your view, with the history of Asian settlement in the
United States, or is it an aberrant story, something that
really wasn't in the American past?*

The internment of Japanese and Japanese Americans,
which took place right after Pearl Harbor, was a more
traumatic event in terms of anti-Japanese, anti-Asian
feeling than anything else we can point to in American
history. But it was not alone. There has always been
anti-immigrant feeling in the United States. We had
the Chinese Exclusion Act, which was passed in the
late nineteenth century to keep the Chinese out of the
country. And Asians had always faced discrimination in
this country in the late nineteenth and early twentieth
centuries.

So what happened in World War II was not an isolat-
ed fact, but the attack on Pearl Harbor created a special situation of hysteria in which the War Department
falsified information to suggest that all Japanese on the

West Coast might be couriers and spies giving signals to Japanese naval vessels.

One of the most terrible things of Roosevelt's administration was the order he signed to remove these Japanese families, to uproot them from their homes on the West Coast, 110,000 of them, and put them in these camps.

It was certainly not an event in American history to make us proud. It was one of the events of World War II that might lead you to at least question the purity of that war.

Here is a war fought against Hitler, one of the great racists of history, and yet the United States in fighting this war committed this racist act of putting these hundred thousand and more people in these camps. And in the midst of this war, black soldiers were segregated from white soldiers.

I was in the Air Force, and I confess that I wasn't conscious of racial segregation, until one day in basic training at Jefferson Barracks, in Missouri, I suddenly found myself in the midst of black soldiers. They had been invisible to me in the way that black people are so often invisible to white people.

What happened to the Japanese, and the segregation of black people—these things made me begin to question more and more the whole notion of a Good War.

I was a bombardier in the war. I had just come back from England; the war was over in Europe, and I and my crew were slated to go to Japan. I had a thirty-day leave and had been married just before I went overseas and my wife and I were going on a little vacation. We stopped near a bus stop, and there was this headline, ATOMIC BOMB DROPPED ON HIROSHIMA. I remember my feeling at the time: *Well, this is good. This will end the war. I won't have to go to Japan, and I won't have to fly missions in Asia.*

Well, after the war, I read John Hersey's book *Hiroshima*. He had gone into Hiroshima and interviewed the survivors of the atomic bomb. You can imagine what those survivors looked like. They were people without arms, people without legs; they were blind; they were people whose skin you could not bear to look at.

He had talked to these people and described what they told him. He was a wonderful journalist, and as I read this for the first time, I who had dropped bombs on various cities in Europe, for the first time I realized what bombing does to human beings. I began to think about what had happened to people when I dropped those bombs, because when you fly at thirty thousand feet, as we did over cities in Europe, you don't see anything down below. You don't see human beings. You don't see blood. You don't hear screams. You don't see kids with their limbs torn off. It is possible not to really understand what you are doing.

I then began to look into the bombing of cities in Europe. I learned that the bombing of civilian populations was deliberate. There was a deliberate strategy to bomb the working-class districts of cities, to destroy the morale of the German people. And that is why sixty thousand people could be killed in one raid in Hamburg or Frankfurt, and perhaps a hundred thousand in Dresden in the spring of 1945.

The work of the historian is to see the world from thirty thousand feet and *the world at ground level, together, and make some sort of coherent understanding out of it. You think with regret about the work you did in World War II, but wasn't it necessary to win the war? Should you have not bombed those places? Should we have not defeated Hitler? I'm not sure I understand what the final moral count is.*

Well, I don't agree with the moral calculus that says this was terrible, and that was terrible, and this was intolerable, but it had to be done. I think it's more complicated than that. When people want me to give a very simple judgment, after putting all of the evidence together—Was it good? Was it bad? Was it justified? Was it unjustified? I cannot give that simple judgment.

What I *can* say is that I refuse simply to push all of that aside and say, "Well, it was necessary," as people push Hiroshima and Nagasaki aside and say, "Oh, they were necessary." When I actually looked into whether Hiroshima and Nagasaki were necessary, I found they weren't necessary.

Was Hitler evil? Of course, and Mussolini was evil, and the Japanese Empire was evil. Yet that should not lead to the acceptance of the huge number of atrocities we committed. And that is what we were doing; we were committing atrocities. We probably killed six hundred thousand ordinary Germans. They weren't Hitler. They were ordinary Germans.

We killed an equal number, probably six hundred thousand Japanese civilians. We killed a hundred thousand ordinary Japanese men, women, and children in Tokyo in one firebombing. When you add all of that up and you say, "Well, but it had to be done because we had to beat Hitler"—I don't think we can come to that simple a judgment.

I think we have to reconsider it, not because we can go back in time and change history, but so that we don't today make the error of looking at atrocities that we may commit when we bomb cities in the Middle East, or that we committed when we bombed people in Vietnam, and say, "Well, it had to be done in Vietnam to stop communism," or "It has to be done in the Middle East to stop terrorism." I think we need to reconsider World War II because we have to learn something about the world today and how we're behaving today.

I came out of that war and at a certain point, I came to the conclusion that war itself should not be tolerated, not even a so-called Good War, not even a war against an evil enemy. Because war is inevitably the indiscriminate killing of large numbers of innocent people, and I don't think it can be morally justified.

Now sure, evil has to be resisted, it's true, but why should we accept the belief that evil can be resisted only by war? We have seen instances in our own time in which apparently powerful dictatorships have fallen without war. Tyrants die, empires overextend themselves, people rise up in such numbers that dictatorships suddenly topple. Apartheid was done away with in South Africa without the bloody civil war that people very often imagined would have to take place in order to end apartheid. So I don't think we should so easily accept the immorality of our actions and justify them on the grounds that they were necessary to defeat Hitler.

The ratio of civilians killed to military personnel killed has risen constantly since World War II. In World War I, it was probably 90 percent military and 10 percent civilians; in World War II, it was more like 50 percent military and 50 percent civilians. Since then, the ratio has gone up to 80 percent or 85 percent civilians killed in war. That cannot be justified.

Something else occurred to me in the years following World War II, and that is that war is a quick fix. Violence is a way of solving something quickly. It is satisfying in that sense—like a drug. The drug may give you a high, but then you come off it.

I received a letter after World War II from General

George C. Marshall. It's not exactly a personal letter. Sent to 16 million GIs, the letter said, "Congratulations, we have won the war—it will be a new world." But it wasn't a new world. Hitler and Mussolini were gone, but fascism, dictatorships, and military autocracies still existed all over the world. Racism was not gone from the world, and war certainly was not gone.

So I came to the conclusion that we can no longer accept war as a way of solving problems. In fact, you might say that this is the great challenge before the human race in our time: how to solve problems of tyranny, aggression, and injustice without killing huge numbers of people.

Are you suggesting in your view of World War II that, despite our memory of it as a war that united all Americans, the resistance you see throughout American history didn't stop in the 1940s? Are you suggesting that there was no national consensus during World War II?

I think there was a national consensus in support of World War II among Americans, but the extent of that consensus changed over time. Let's put it another way. At the beginning of the war, even after the war had started in Europe, most Americans did not want anything to do with it. There was a fundamental repugnance against war unless you feel you're defending yourself. Roosevelt ran for office in 1940 on a pledge that he would not bring the United States into war.

But then the Japanese attacked Pearl Harbor, creating an atmosphere of fear, which created the possibility then for mobilizing a country that had been reluctant to go to war.

There were still people who didn't go along with the war, people from different sides of the political spectrum. There were America Firsters, a right-wing group who thought that the United States should not get involved. There were pro-Nazi sympathizers, the German American Bund, active in the United States, which was actually admiring of Hitler. Then on the extreme other side, there were pacifists, people who simply did not believe in war. Several thousand pacifists who refused to be drafted went to prison during World War II.

The Communist Party was in support of the war, but there was another, smaller left-wing group, the Trotskyists or Socialist Workers Party, who were opposed to the war. Some of them were in fact prosecuted and sent to prison because of their opposition.

I think it's fair to say it was probably the most popular war in American history. There was more dissension, more disagreement in the Revolutionary War than in World War II.

And it has remained the most popular war. When Studs Terkel did his oral histories of veterans and other people who lived in that period, he called his book *"The Good War"*—and if you look closely, you'll see he put quotation marks around "Good War," because when he actually talked to people, he found it wasn't unanimous.

I have found in speaking to people all over the country that it is very hard to talk about World War II and say anything critical about it. Yet there are people who served in the war who have written to me to say, "You know, I feel the way that you do." There is a man who lives in Denver who was badly wounded in World War II in Europe, and he wrote to me to say, "I just don't believe in war anymore." So there are individuals who question the simple goodness of that war—and of any war, really.

I think the most hurtful legacy of the war is that the memory of the "Good War" has been used to justify *any* war. That's the most dangerous thing about the memory of World War II. We can't do anything about World War II anymore. It's gone. Good or bad, it's gone. But its recollection as a Good War has been used to create analogies, to say our enemy today is like Hitler. Ho Chi Minh is like Hitler. Noriega is like Hitler. Saddam Hussein is like Hitler. And not to fight is like being Neville Chamberlain and appeasing. All these analogies to World War II are ways of getting people to support war, even though the situations are very different from World War II.

The pattern in your storytelling about American history seems to feature a certain amount of pushback from rank-and-file Americans, which is then suppressed. Pushback, suppression. The suppression of slave revolts. The flowering of Reconstruction and then its suppression. The use of World War I to suppress various radical movements in the interwar period. Does World War II fall into that pattern? Was there a way in which World War II gave those in power the upper hand to push back down on things that were happening during the Great Depression?

War gives the government an opportunity to do what it would like to do all the time—to control oppositional movements and suppress dissonant opinion. This was true of World War II also.

We saw that in the Cold War, too, after the Soviet Union rose out of World War II to rival the power of the United States. The existence of the Soviet Union and the exaggerated threat of communism created an atmosphere that enabled the government, even under Truman, to compel government employees to sign loyalty oaths in order to attain their jobs. The FBI's powers expanded enormously. We put people in jail for refusing to talk to congressional committees about their political affiliations.

This raises the prospect of a government that assumes dictatorial power over the thinking of the population, and dictatorial control of the population—with defense of this control resting on the idea that we are in danger and therefore cannot have the democratic liberties that you think the Bill of Rights gives us.

War is a poisoning of the mind. War poisons everybody who is engaged in it.

* * *

In recounting these episodes and the long haul of American history, you have delivered a pretty tough critique of this country and its past. Is there any country that has gotten it right? Is there any country that's delivered justice to its people and security to its workers? One that's been fair where you have seen the United States as being unfair?

When you criticize the government of the United States harshly as I've done, criticize its foreign and domestic policy, you are asked the question, "Do you know of a better place?" The assumption is that, if all other places in the world are flawed, if you can't find a really good society, then we must be the best. I don't accept that. I don't think there is a really good society anywhere in the world. We live in a world of imperfect societies. There are terrible societies. There are places that are much more repressive of their populations than the United States, and certainly there are places that have much more severe poverty than the United States.

However, there are also places that have *better* social systems, that have better health systems than the United States. There are countries that take better care of their children, their old people, and their unemployed.

And if you look at the figures given out by the United Nations, by the World Health Organization, you'll find that in the ranking of countries with fair health programs, programs that will take care of the poor as well as the rich, the United States ranks twentieth in the world. In infant mortality, there are twenty-five countries that have lower rates of infant mortality. One out of every five children in the United States is born poor. There are countries with much better literacy rates than the United States.

Of course, there are many countries that are worse.

We have over 2 million people in prison in the United States. We have the highest rate of incarceration of any country in the world. There must be something wrong when you have 2 million people in prison, plus another 6 to 8 million people who have been in prison or are on probation.

There is another way in which the United States is probably worse than any other country in the world at present, and that is the extent to which it has used its military power to invade other countries and to kill faraway people who are no threat to us. The U.S. government has been doing this ever since the Spanish-American War.

My point is that I don't think it's necessary to find a

totally good society somewhere in the world in order to be critical of what we have in the United States. I don't think we should measure ourselves against dictatorships. We should measure ourselves against an ideal, against what we would like our country to be.

You are not anti-American when you criticize the United States. It is part of democracy to live in this country and to be critical of what you see, as well.

If you were to give us a short action plan, what are some of the things that you would like to see the country do, to do better by its poor people, by its working people?

We are a very rich country, and I believe there are things we can do that we haven't done. We can have free universal health care for everybody—and I don't mean one of these complicated health-care systems like the one Hillary Clinton proposed in 1993, a thousand pages long and designed to keep the insurance companies in the game.

I don't mean the present system. I don't mean any health system where you have to deal with insurance companies, make co-payments, or fill out forms. When I talk about a universal health-care system, I think of the time that I was in Air Force training and caught pneumonia out in

California. There were no antibiotics at that time, but they had just discovered sulfa drugs. I was close to death, but sulfa drugs saved me.

I didn't have to fill out forms. I didn't have to pay any money. People in the military get good free medical care. Why can't everybody get this? Sure, the government has to pay, but it's a simple, clear, efficient, egalitarian system, and everybody gets medical care.

There are countries where this is true. I got sick in Italy, and even though I was a foreigner, I was getting free medical care. I was in France, and the same thing happened to me. We could afford it if we weren't spending $500 billion a year on war and military preparations.

We could afford it if we had a truly progressive income tax, not the tax system we have now, in which wealth rises toward the top because of the tax breaks at the top. If we had a truly progressive tax system, we would be freeing hundreds of billions of dollars a year that we could spend on universal health care. We could spend some of it on guaranteeing paid work to people who lose their jobs. The government *could* do what the New Deal did in 1930s—provide jobs to the unemployed. We have the money, but we're just wasting it—wasting it on war, wasting it by giving it to the richest 1 percent of the population.

*　*　*

After you learned about the violent, ugly events leading up to the Revolution—the massacre of the Indians, the diaries of de las Casas and the oppression of Columbus, mutiny, class conflict, Shays' Rebellion—why didn't you just walk away from the research and pick a new topic? This is pretty grim stuff.

It *is* grim stuff, and yet there is another side to it. There are always people who recognize what is wrong and try to do something about it. De las Casas doing something to expose Columbus. People in the Revolutionary Army mutinying against the conditions that the privates endured. The rebels of Shays' Rebellion, the small farmers, acting out of their needs. That is what has inspired me.

When you think about the events of the first half of the twentieth century—the movement against World War I, the Tulsa Race Riot, Helen Keller's outspokenness, postwar black organizing, Frank Emi and the Japanese internment—does it get more difficult because you

actually have personal memories of some of these his-
toric events and saw some of them? Is it harder to get the
necessary distance?

I guess I don't want distance (*laughs*). I've never thought
that distance gives you a truer picture. In fact, I've always
thought the opposite. I thought that the closer you could
get to a story, the more you were personally involved in it,
the more truths you'd find that you would not get at a distance. It has been a greater education for me to combine
the history I read in books *with* the history I've experi-
enced in my own life.

So it's not more difficult to separate out your own feel-
ings, to open yourself up to new truths about things that
you remember personally?

I would like to think that, although I have had forma-
tive experiences—in the Depression, World War II, and
the postwar period—I like to think that I've been listen-
ing to other people, also.

If other people have experiences different from mine, I
want to listen to theirs. I don't want to have a view of history that's narrowed by my own relationship to it. It's a

challenge to do that—to combine the memories of others with your own memory and come out, not with a simple picture but with a more complex picture.

I think people who haven't looked deeply into the history of both the civil rights movement and the labor movement might assume that they are natural allies. Have they been? Have there been moments when black workers have had to demand that the labor movement recognize them and understand their struggle?

There has been a very complex relationship between black people and white people in the labor movement. When the CIO [Congress of Industrial Organizations] rose as a rebel organization in the labor movement in the 1930s, it did what the AF of L [American Federation of Labor] never succeeded in doing—organizing black workers and bringing them together with white workers. This happened in the rubber plants and the auto plants and steel plants, and you saw black and white workers getting together in the meat-packing industry, and forming these new industrial unions, which carried on the great strikes of the 1930s.

When I was eighteen and nineteen years old, working in the Brooklyn Navy Yard, black people as well as unskilled white people were not allowed into the AF of L craft meetings. And black people were assigned the toughest jobs. But I am very impressed with the fact that there are certain times in history when the divisions between black people and white people are overcome and they work together against a common enemy.

In Tennessee, the Highlander Folk School was a sort of oddity in the South, a little oasis in the midst of racial segregation where black people and white people got together, went to classes together, and studied history together. There working people and trade unionists, black and white, met in, you might say, a little protected enclave in the South. That to me was a glimpse of what might be possible.

What was the Dodge Revolutionary Union Movement (DRUM)?

The Dodge Revolutionary Movement was a movement mostly of black workers in the Dodge plants in the auto industry who became convinced that they had to organize themselves.

It was an instance of what became known as Black

Power—the belief that black people had to organize their own groups in order to defend their rights, that white people would dominate integrated groups and the interests of black people would be subordinated. They were a force and an inspiration to black workers.

But did that hinder the work of the UAW, which was trying to represent war workers in the auto union, in the auto industry?

I think it was temporarily troublesome for the United Auto Workers. In the short run, it created some dissension and hostility. But I think in the longer run, it had a positive effect, in making white workers more conscious of the needs of black workers, more conscious of the need for equal pay for black and white workers.

Separatist movements, while they are not the solution for the human race, very often serve a function of at least temporarily giving a kind of self-respect and dignity to people who have been overlooked. This was true of DRUM, and it was true of the black separatist movement of the 1960s and 1970s.

* * *

Moving on to the Vietnam War, was there frequent rebel-lion in the ranks of soldiers fighting in Southeast Asia? Was there resistance there as in other wars?

There was probably more resistance to the Vietnam War in the military ranks than to any other war in American history. It is hard to measure, because there were no large-scale mutinies as in the Revolutionary War.

Rebellion in the ranks of the soldiers in Vietnam was continuous as the war went on, as it became more unpopular at home, as the number of casualties grew, and as recognition spread that there was something wrong with this war. There were hundreds of fragging incidents, in which GIs rolled grenades under the tents of their officers—and this is something that most Americans to this day know very little about.

Rebellion took many forms. It took the form of soldiers taking drugs; it took the form of desertions, a remarkable number of desertions. It took the form of soldiers refusing to go out in the field, of soldiers wearing black armbands to signify their solidarity with the antiwar movement at home.

This revolt inside the ranks then manifested itself when these veterans came back from Vietnam and formed a group called Vietnam Veterans Against the War. They assembled at the Capitol in Washington in 1971, when the war was still going on, and they threw their medals over a fence into a pile, to dramatize their opposition to the war.

The movement against the Vietnam War is seen as a student movement, but if there is any one factor that may have been most important in making the U.S. government realize that it could not carry on the war, it was an army that was becoming more and more rebellious.

Thirty years after the evacuation of Saigon, you can still get into a pretty good argument about whether the United States was defeated in Vietnam, but whatever it was, it certainly wasn't a victory. Did the U.S. government learn anything from that experience?

I think the U.S. government learned a lot from that experience. I think it was forced to learn. After all, it was confronting a situation that was hardly to be believed. The United States was always the victor in war. And here we had actually lost one. We have to admit that.

I think this caused a lot of reflection in high government circles. They didn't want to give up the idea of American military intervention in other parts of the world, and yet they didn't want the same thing to happen that happened in Vietnam. And so what they learned from the Vietnam War was that if they were going to have more military interventions, they had better be short. They'd better not last long enough for an antiwar movement to develop.

It took several years before the American public turned against the war. When the war began in 1965, two-thirds of the American people supported the war. Three years later, two-thirds of the American people *opposed* the war. That was a very dramatic turnaround.

So the government decided that we're going to have short wars. We are going to have "splendid little wars"—and what could be shorter than President Reagan's war in Grenada?

It was almost laughable that this tiny Caribbean island was perceived as a threat to the United States. All sorts of propaganda disseminated by the United States said it was going to be used as a Cuban or Soviet military base. Alternatively, the invasion was explained as a way to save Americans who were in the medical school and had to be evacuated, and so on.

How much military resistance are they going to get on the island of Grenada? Virtually none—it was a great military victory.

There was a short war in Panama under George Bush Sr. Then in 1991, a very short war against Iraq, lasting a couple of months. So they learned from the Vietnam War that you mustn't give the American population a chance to think about what is happening and to reconsider whether the reasons the government is giving you for the war are valid.

One of the other things they learn from the Vietnam War is that they must do a better job of selling the war to the American people, and to do that they must have better control over the information that becomes public. In Grenada, Panama, and Iraq, they made great attempts to control the information that was given out by journalists to the American public. In the current war in Iraq, they did a very interesting thing. They decided to entice journalists into believing that they would get a better story if they embedded themselves in the American military. This is a way of suggesting to reporters that they'll get a more accurate story because they will be right there in the middle of things, but it's also a way of controlling them.

But for all the dismay and the regrouping that had to be done inside American institutions after the Vietnam

War, there would seem to be no question that America still reserved to itself the right to remove governments, to go beyond its shores, and to use military force around the world.

That is absolutely true. The government was not going to be daunted by its loss in Vietnam. If the United States government was going to remain a world power, we would need to feel free to intervene in the affairs of other countries.

But I also think that one of the lessons learned from the Vietnam War is to avoid intervening overtly with military force. If possible, do it surreptitiously—do it covertly.

In 1976 the report of the Church Committee of the Senate included a volume called *Covert Action in Chile 1963–1973*. The United States did not like the government of Chile. Chile had elected a socialist named Salvador Allende. Instead of sending a military force, as we had done again and again in Latin America in the early part of the century, and later in Vietnam, the Nixon administration decided to overthrow the Allende government by covert action—by secret actions to support the opposition and encourage a military coup. In 1973, the coup succeeded, and Allende was overthrown.

Covert action became notorious when the Reagan administration gave support to the counter-revolutionaries in Nicaragua, who were working to overthrow the left-wing revolutionary government that had taken power in Nicaragua in 1979.

Beginning in 1946, the United States openly operated the U.S. Army School of the Americas [in 2001 renamed the Western Hemisphere Institute for Security Cooperation] to train officers from armies throughout the hemisphere—to professionalize those forces and keep the soldiers in their barracks instead of in the presidential palace, as well as to regularize what it means to be a soldier elsewhere in the hemisphere. Has it worked?

The School of the Americas actually started in Panama and then was moved to Fort Benning, Georgia. It has been a way for the United States to exercise even more control over Latin America than it had in the past.

The real reason for the school is not simply training, but to send back into their countries a group of officers who have been indoctrinated in an American school, who will be from that point on in touch with the American government, and perhaps ready to do its bidding. When somebody pointed out that many of the leaders of the Chile coup had been graduates of the School of the Americas, the head of the school said in effect, "Well, we keep in touch with our graduates, and they keep in touch with us."

* * *

One hundred forty years or so after the removal of American Indians from the southeastern United States, after the Trail of Tears, and after the Jacksonian approach toward Indians in white-settled areas, there is an American Indian movement again in the United States. What does that tell us?

This is one of the most fascinating developments of the last few decades. The Indian population had been nearly annihilated in the massacres of the nineteenth century and had been pushed into Indian territory in Oklahoma, then pushed out of Indian territory when oil was discovered there. Then in the 1960s, an Indian movement formed—AIM, the American Indian Movement. They engaged in acts of resistance. They did dramatic actions. They took over the island of Alcatraz. They went to Wounded Knee, the site of the last great massacre of Indians, in 1890, and they occupied it until they were routed by federal forces.

AIM made themselves visible in the way that black people made themselves visible in the civil rights movement.

* * *

Speaking of movements in the 1960s, one of the most important to arise during that time is the lesbian, gay, bisexual, transgender rights movement. The early years of ACT UP (AIDS Coalition to Unleash Power), in the 1980s, may be the first time that people really took notice. But what was happening before that?

I think one of the most extraordinary developments in the 1960s was the very slow, almost invisible change in attitude about sexual orientation. If you go back a century, there is a history of black resistance, the labor movement, antiwar activity—but no real history of a gay rights movement.* I have no doubt that the lesbian, gay, bisexual, transgender, and queer rights movement was encouraged by the existence of other rights movements, but it was something that was new on the American scene, and at times it took dramatic form. Like the incident at Stonewall, where people from the LGBTQ community

---

* There are of course now any number of powerful histories of the gay rights movement available.

got together and rebelled against their treatment by the police. The culture began to change. And I think this was part of and connected with the new freedoms of the 1960s, a greater willingness to talk about sex and sexual orientation, and an openness about things that you couldn't talk about before. That has been, I think, one of the most remarkable developments of these past decades.

*   *   *

There have been Spanish-speaking people in what is now the United States for five hundred years, but the Latino movement seems to be a fairly late comer to the American tradition of pushback and resistance. Why?

The Latino movement took a while to become part of the general movement of revolt that we saw throughout American society in the 1960s. To a great extent, that's because Latinos were very often segregated, the work that they did was unrecognized, and they were kind of a submerged part of the population. They first burst upon the American scene in an important way in the late 1960s, when farmworkers out in California began to organize.

The name of Cesar Chavez is an important name in the history of American social movements. He was one of the leaders of a new movement among Latino farmworkers in the West—a particularly charismatic and effective leader.

This was something unusual for migrant workers, separated from other people by language, and so many of them were undocumented. Moreover, they faced a very powerful farming industry, agribusiness, the great food corporations.

But they began to organize in the 1960s, and they succeeded in forcing these very powerful corporations to deal with them. One of the ways they did it was by organizing a boycott of grapes. This was a technique that had not been used in such a dramatic way in America for a long time, but it was remarkably successful. They appealed to people all over the country to support them. And I think the fact that other people in the country were involved in other movements of protest against the establishment helped create an atmosphere in which people observed the boycott.

The thing about rich corporations is that, powerful as they are, a boycott that cuts into their profits is something that they will listen to. The result was that the farmworkers on the West Coast organized successfully and won victories and managed to make some change in their conditions.

In thinking of the role of the Latino people as part of

the general wave of movements in the 1960s, we should point out that they were an unnoticed part of the antiwar movement. On the West Coast, there were demonstrations involving thousands of Latinos and Latinas protesting against the war in Vietnam.

We now are becoming more aware of Latino organization and resistance, and I think maybe part of the reason is that we have more Latino people here. You can see this in the arguments over bilingualism. To me, this is all a positive development.

*   *   *

How do these more recent stories and movements help connect the modern decades with our earlier history?

What we have today is the continuation of the struggles that we have had all through American history, taking different forms and with movements maybe not as visible and strong as they have been in the past, but the conflicts are still there—that is, the conflicts among classes and between the interests of the rich and the interests of the poor.

The struggle may take different forms than it did with the strikes of the 1930s. The struggle may take the form of a conflict over the tax system. And I suspect it will continue to go on, so long as we have a country that's very rich, most of whose wealth is used for things that do not make life better for most people in this country.

The movement against the war in Iraq was in many ways a continuation of that long history of movements against war—a movement against poor young people being sent to war, being enticed into the army by promises, and propagandized into the military by talk of democracy and liberty being brought to other countries. That struggle against war and against militarism continues today.

The women's movement today is organized in a different way—and perhaps not as well organized as the women's movement of the 1960s and 1970s, but there is certainly a movement among women today, for instance, to defend the right of abortion.

The labor movement today is much weaker than it has been in the past. We had as much as 30 percent of the labor force organized in the 1930s; now we have perhaps 12 percent of the labor force organized. Yet there are still labor struggles going on in this country. There are still strikes going on. Some of them lose; some of them win. We have nurses going out on strike; we have janitors going out on strike. We have campus workers on colleges and universities throughout the country demanding a living wage.

Although we certainly are not seeing the great wave of protest that we saw during the Vietnam era, during the civil rights era, the struggles still continue—rich against poor, antiwar people against the war makers, women against the special form of subjection and intimate oppression that takes place in families and in society. We are still seeing a population that will not simply accept what they perceive to be injustice.

* * *

You write often of the possibilities for surprise that A People's History *can show us. In all these stories, is there embedded the idea that the people who read the book are themselves actors in history. Is it an implicit call to action, to get people to think in a different way about themselves and their role in the life of the country?*

I suppose that it might be considered an unprofessional thing for a historian to write a history that somebody else interprets as a call to action. But to me, the historian is a citizen before he is a historian. The historian is a human being before he is a historian.

He is not a historian, in my view, just to be a historian—just to teach history, just to write books, just to go to professional meetings. I assume that a historian is somebody who cares about what is going on in the world, someone who studies history and teaches history and writes about history in a way that will have a beneficial effect on the world.

I have said that there is no such thing as being neutral in writing history, no such thing as being objective. And there's no such thing as staying apart from the conflicts that there are in the world. In fact, it is not only undesirable to do that, but it is really impossible to do that, because the world is already moving in certain directions. To pretend to neutrality—to stand off, to say things and do things and write things that will not have an effect—is to deceive yourself.

What you are doing, then, is allowing the world to go on without your intervention. I see the historian as somebody who intervenes, whose work should lead other people to think that they are not simply passive instruments. If you tell the history of the United States as a history of presidents and Congresses and Supreme Court justices and military leaders and "important people," you are telling your readers that these are the people who make history, and their job is simply to go to the polls every four years and elect a leader who will take care of them. That to me is a crippling of democracy. Democracy requires an active citizenry. Therefore, you might say the writing of history should itself be a democratic act. It should promote democracy by giving people the idea that they too can participate in history.

In fact, they had better participate in history, because if they leave the decisions to the people who now run the society, we will just have endless wars. We will have an endless class struggle in which the rich increase their wealth, and the poor in this country and other countries have a hard time to survive.

You write that history suggests new definitions of power. How does looking back at the past shine that kind of light into the future?

What we learn from history about power is that power is not what we have always thought it to be, or what on the surface it seems to be. That is, if you have the most money and the most guns, you have the most power. And if you control the media, you certainly have the most power.

What history shows is that people who seemed to have

no power—who did not have the money, people who did not have military forces at their disposal, who did not control the means of communication—were able nevertheless at certain points in history to change their lives because they found their own kind of power—the power of organized people.

They found that if the people who are troubled by their lives organize in enough numbers and persist long enough, and are willing to take enough risks, they can overcome the people who seem to have all the power.

We have seen this in the labor movement. How are workers going to win the eight-hour day in the nineteenth century? They don't have the power the corporations have. The government is not on their side. They don't have political power. There is nothing in the Constitution that requires employers to limit workdays to eight hours. The workers don't have the army or the police on their side. But they have this kind of power—if they get together, if they organize, they can stop the machinery of production by going on strike. That is a power that the corporation must recognize.

Even though the corporation may try everything it can, bringing in strikebreakers, bringing in the police and the army, if the strikers persist—if they actually succeed in really diminishing the profits of the corporation, in preventing the factories from running—they have succeeded in forcing these apparently powerful corporations to change their ways.

When workers in the auto industry in the 1930s struck against Ford and General Motors, many people said they would never win. You couldn't win against Ford or GM. They had too much money, too much force on their side. And the government was not going to help you either. The police were not going to help you. But workers discovered that if they stuck together and persisted, they were creating a power that had to be recognized.

And the same thing is true of black people in the South. I could see this firsthand when I moved south, to Atlanta, Georgia, in 1956. Who were more powerless than black people in the South? They had nobody on the police force, no mayors, nobody in the state legislatures. They had no political power. They certainly had very, very little economic power. They were the poorest part of the population. They did not even have the federal government on their side, even though we had the Fourteenth and

Fifteenth Amendments and constitutionally the federal government was supposed to enforce these and make sure that black people could vote, that they were not discriminated against. The federal government was not doing any of that.

Black people in 1950s and 1960s in the South decided they had to do it on their own. They had to organize themselves.

They boycotted the buses in Montgomery. They began to demonstrate all over the South, and the word of what they were doing began to get out. The media—even though it was not particularly sympathetic to black people—the media was sympathetic to dramatic news stories. The media began to cover the demonstrations, and the pictures were seen all over the world. The U.S. government became embarrassed by the pictures of black people being beaten by police and being driven back by fire hoses. So black people discovered that they had a power that could change things—and they did change things. Things changed in the South. And the federal government changed, Congress changed, the president changed.

We had a president who was a Southerner and who

had never been particularly sympathetic to the movement going on national radio and saying the anthem of the civil rights movement, "We Shall Overcome."

And the movement against the Vietnam War showed the power of people to cause a government to move away from a war. I remember the beginnings of the antiwar movement. As we protested against the war in early 1965, when the escalation of the war began significantly, we thought, *How in the world are we going to have an effect on government policy? They have the power; we don't.* But in fact, our power grew as more and more people joined the antiwar movement.

Truth has a power of its own. The truth about the war in Vietnam became clearer and clearer to more and more people.

I spoke at an antiwar rally in Boston on the Boston Common in early 1965, and I think there were perhaps a hundred people there. Four years later, in 1969, I spoke at another rally on the Boston Common; there were a hundred thousand people there.

The movement grew to a point where the government had to pay attention to it. And the movement extended to people who are never expected to be rebellious, to priests and nuns and rabbis and businessmen and people in all walks of life.

Organization, persistence, moral fervor, commitment —those are elements of a different kind of power.

* * *

The stories you've just recounted, and the ones you have spun out from the history of the fifteenth to the twenty-first centuries—do they leave you optimistic about the future of this country?

I would be naive if I said I'm confident that this country has a glorious future, based on the past.

Nevertheless, the future is open. I would say I'm not optimistic and not pessimistic. I would say I'm cautiously hopeful. I think it depends so much on what people do and how fast and how seriously people organize to change their lives. But the element of optimism in my feeling comes from faith in people's essential decency.

I don't think people want war. I don't think people are born racists. I think people are basically decent, but their decency can be twisted and distorted by people in power who will create reasons for them to go to war, or will persuade them that free-market capitalism is the best system ever devised.

It takes time, but I believe that the truth—even though it emerges only slowly and over a long period—does have a power of its own.

And I expect that power to become more and more crucial. I am hopeful that people will turn against the idea of war. I think the point will come when people will finally say, "We can't go to war anymore. It hasn't done us any good."

There are people everywhere who want to see a different kind of world, who want to be at one with their fellow men and women, who think that people in other countries are human beings as we are, and that if somebody is suffering anywhere in the world, we have a responsibility to help them.

I believe that that compassion is basic to human nature. And I am counting on that to pull us through.

INDEX

ABOUT THE AUTHORS

Howard Zinn (1922–2010) was a historian, playwright, and activist and the author of numerous books, including the bestselling *A People's History of the United States*. He received the Lannan Literary Award for nonfiction and the Eugene V. Debs Award for his writing and political activism.

Ray Suarez is co-host of the public radio program and podcast *World Affairs*. He was chief national correspondent for *PBS NewsHour* and the host of *Talk of the Nation* on NPR. He is the author of several books, including *Latino Americans*. He lives in Philadelphia and Washington.

FILM CREDITS FOR HOWARD ZINN: THE PEOPLE'S HISTORIAN

HISTORIAN

Howard Zinn

INTERVIEWER

Ray Suarez

EXECUTIVE PRODUCER

Alvin H. Perlmutter

DIRECTOR

Christopher Lukas

PRODUCER

Lisa Zbar

FILM CREDITS

INTERVIEW PRODUCER

Lorne Lieb

LEAD CAMERA

Greg Barna

ADDITIONAL CAMERA

David Smith

Tom Mason

SOUND

John Duvall

PRODUCTION MANAGER/SOUND

John Schwally

PRODUCTION ASSISTANT

Joseph Schroeder

MAKEUP/HAIR

Kelly MacNeal

With the permission of the Estate of Howard Zinn

PUBLISHING IN THE PUBLIC INTEREST

Thank you for reading this book published by The New Press. The New Press is a nonprofit, public interest publisher. New Press books and authors play a crucial role in sparking conversations about the key political and social issues of our day.

We hope you enjoyed this book and that you will stay in touch with The New Press. Here are a few ways to stay up to date with our books, events, and the issues we cover:

- Sign up at www.thenewpress.com/subscribe to receive updates on New Press authors and issues and to be notified about local events
- Like us on Facebook: www.facebook.com/newpressbooks
- Follow us on Twitter: www.twitter.com/thenewpress

Please consider buying New Press books for yourself; for friends and family; or to donate to schools, libraries, community centers, prison libraries, and other organizations involved with the issues our authors write about.

The New Press is a 501(c)(3) nonprofit organization. You can also support our work with a tax-deductible gift by visiting www.thenewpress.com/donate.